I0766966

NO MORE BROKEN SLATE

NO MORE BROKEN SLATE

Suresh Kolhe

Notion Press

Old No. 38, New No. 6
McNichols Road, Chetpet
Chennai - 600 031

First Published by Notion Press 2016
Copyright © Suresh Kolhe 2016
All Rights Reserved.

ISBN 978-1-946280-30-5

Dedicated To

My Family,

Mother Smt. Laxmi Mata

Wife Anita

Daughters Ruby & Supriya

Son Aditya, & daughter in law Priyanka

Son In Laws Sachin & Abhijit

Grand daughters Sara & Radha– Rani,

Sau. Mai & Shri Bhausaheb Vikhe (Patil) of Loni.

(Who all have always borne with me in distress !)
and Nevertheless every farmer
(who is my true idol).

"Inspirations"

1. BABAJI, alias late Janardan Swamiji

   *Whose selfless work inspired me to write about his teachings in my maiden attempt (yet to be published) - **The Saint with the rusted throne.** ("Captioned… Give me your sufferings")*

2. My Father Late G.K. Kolhe.

   Born a farmer,… Died a farmer !

   Illiterate by times, he listened more &spoke less only to glow with wisdom. (Truly a seasoned man that I always wished to be).

3. Shri Bhau, – My Eldest Brother (Shri Shankarraoji Kolhe Saheb)

   A man for all seasons!

   Today – even at 88, he talks of Co-generation, Quality education, Bio Technology and Revolt against injustice.

   He mastered the craft of Politics upon his return from the State College, Utah, USA in mid 1950's – & laddered up to be the gem of the National Sugar Cooperatives.

4. Mr. S.S. Patil, Pune (ex.CEO–Kirlosker Cummins Ltd.)

   Who always impressed me with his strength of words & punctuality.

5. My Colleague-

   B Chandrasekhar of Warangal- whose daily life saving messages kept me rolling over the bad patches of life.

1. Babaji

2. Late G.K Kolhe

3. S.G. Kolhe

From thumb print...   to   The Mega center for Learning!

THE SANJIVANI EDUCATION FOUNDATION, KOPARGAON (M.S.)
(The Journey like never before)

Contents

Foreword xi

The Book xiii

Special Acknowledgements xv

Prologue xvii

Moreover, the Book xix

Global Warming xxi

Modest Appeal xxv

A few lines from the chapter-The Global Warming xxvii

Few lines from the Chapter, The Thorny - Trail xxix

The Grim Reality, LAND– the reservoir, AGRICULTURE – the pump! xxx

The Thorny Trail xxxii

PART 1

1. The Thorny Trail! 3

2. The Dream Forbidden 5

3. Global Warming 14

4. Agriculture & Banking! 32

5. Caution: This road leads to a dead end 43

6. The Agony- (The Grim Reality) 54

PART 2

1. The Hope   65

2. Capsule growing   76

3. The Golden Ridge   87

4. Eradication of Global Warming - The dream!   97

5. The Festive Aura of Agriculture   104

About Myself   *117*

Bibliography   *119*

Foreword

Ever since the man opted - chiseling the top soil with **sharpened** stones,

................agonies seem to have trailed Agriculture!

The path of progress – can not ignore the price of progress. It would be lethal – if we fail to obey the nature now!

Someone has to spin the wheel of agriculture – the other way around, to bring home, Bees and the Butterflies once again! (We can if we really mean to)

The Book

Journey's you beyond farming - deep into the lives of the toiling peasants.

It Is Not Fiction:

.......But a way out!

It Is Not Escapism:

.......But a prosper theme!

It Holds The Promise Of A New Slate For Sarita!

Special Acknowledgements

1. Esquires book of American Automobiles
2. Several old Auto Car & Car and Driver Issues.
3. The Higher Taste – ISKON
4. 'Nash-Rambler' - A book on Automobile

Prologue

The strength of the Nation comes from the Land and...

" the land is in trouble ! "

Agriculture – the man made Ecological system can no more escape certain Ecological laws – than Newton's apple could ignore the law of gravitation!

This book is about a peasant's struggle to make agriculture ever joyous for ever – on the Golden Ridges-Bio Diversity Farming pattern !

(The Authors Bio-diversity farm being groomed in to an eco tourism venture – 'Nature Station Aditya')

Moreover, the Book

It also ropes in the "Mannat" makers of Bollywood - To adopt orphans like Sarita and heal in turn from their run for the riches!

.... Obliviously, It aims at –making Sarita blush again & dance with the butterflies on the Golden Ridges !

The book truly resonates the evils of Global-Warming into our minds! Agriculture is in doldrums,as monoculture and global warming are supportive to each other. Someone is out 'turning the wheel of Agriculture, the other way around, destined to make our planet a paradise in the galaxy's !

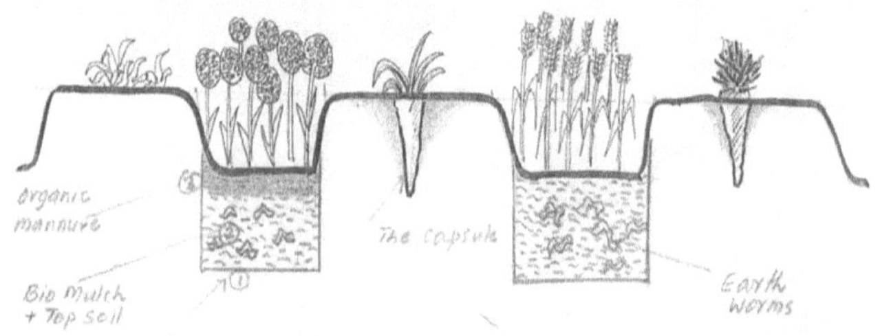

(Golden Ridge – is a unique bio – diversity farming module devised by the author to check Global – warming & bring added sustainability to agriculture in the tropics.)

Global Warming

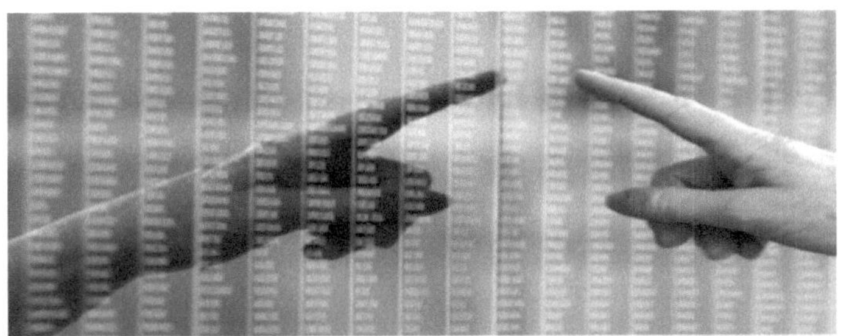

You could be in the list of the Global Warming casualties!

'Tsunami's are now a frequent affair!

'Tornadoes are also common'

(Intensified U.V Rays)

WE MUST TRY HARD TO KEEP THIS MENACE AWAY

– By planting as many trees - all over!

Caution

CLOUD CLOT

HOLLOCAUST

EARTH QUAKES

VOLCANOES

TSUNAMI

TORNADOES

& THE OZONE HOLE

(...They all constitute,the Global Warming Package)

The Volcanoes

The Earthquakes

The Cloudclott

Modest Appeal

"Whenever the land is in trouble – it's inhabitants also live a troublesome life! Let us all confess for fouling the environment and take an oath for its rapid restoration"

"G.K. Memorial – centre for nature care!" Is a public charitable trust committed for the Environmental Protection and is promoted by the author Shri. Suresh Kolhe

A word of appreciation - little donation and plenty of blessings, would take the Trust G.K. Memorial - a long way in enriching the lives of the distressed peasants while restoring the Ecology resourcefully.

Trust Regn. No.E-675

Donation to be in favour of → G K Memorial Centre For Nature Care

Payable at KOPARGAON-423601(M.S.) INDIA

Bank – Sai Sanjivani Co-operative Bank Ltd, Kopargaon

IFSC – HDFC0CSSCBI – 5th letter to be read as zero.

Savings A/c No- 12725

Late Shri Genuji Krishnaji Kolhe (Patil). Though, illiterate by times, he was true ecologist and a naturopath. A loving father and a toiling Peasant,who started a primary school on his farm in early 1950's to educate the children of farm labourers.

Suresh Kolhe, Chief Promoter
(G.K. Memorial Center for Nature Care)

A few lines from the chapter–
The Global Warming

A Caution for all – on Global Warming

**Global-Warming, is the disastrous outcome of
Environmental pollution and continual deforestation!
(It is now,trailing us like our own shadow.)**

Last night – I dream't a horrible dream. It must be little over midnight or so – when, I visualized that the sky had turned dangerously red. The Sun had come up blazing cosmic radiations all over and within a few minutes, the fury started fusing onto our planet.

The turbulent winds started whirling into Tornadoes; the Tidal waves into Tsunami's & the seismic faults into Earthquakes & Volcanoes – engulfing everything that lay in their way.

The birds soon started finding another heavens and the weaker ones - like the Butterflies, went out of breath and fell on the flower beds – dead once for all. The flower-beds in our court-yard also appeared wilted as if no one had watered them for weeks together.

The weary young men on the streets, too-wore wrinkled faces - making them look weird and much older for their age. I got frightened of this ordeal and jumped out of the bed – perhaps to get rid of this satanic dream.

I, then walked a few steps in the darkness towards the window to switch on the light. With the lights on – I found that it were the early hours of  the dawn. I then restlessly – glanced at the flower-bed adjoining the window sill. I was stunned to see the flower that was in full bloom, only the last night – now lay crippled and its petals robbed of the very fragrance. Further, as I looked down – I spotted a beautiful Butterfly lying dead on the floor. This was for real and was perhaps a caution of life for all of us – *"that this nightmare shouldn't be ignored as a mere dream."*

If we do not care for the ecological restoration… now, then we all would have the same fate as the innocent butterfly that lay dead on the floor.

Obviously, - there is only one way out for our survival,

TO WAGE A WAR AGAINST GLOBAL WARMING!!

(………a threat – more alarming than the nuclear war-fare)

Few lines from the Chapter,
The Thorny – Trail
(The Dream Forbidden)

The thought of Sarita's broken – slate, left Ramu-shivering all over, – for he had sensed the defeat of his struggle.

Torn between living and livelihood, he now had only one sad option

….. to bid farewell to the Mother Earth

The Postmortem of his corpse, a few days later - revealed nothing but,

Hunger &

Sorrow!

(Needless to say -the Postmortem of the Society we live in and the Postmortem of our religion and Political bonding may have perhaps quenched the distressed soul to some extent!)

The Grim Reality
LAND– *the reservoir,*
AGRICULTURE – *the pump!*

The demise of a defeated peasant reveals of a flaw in the modern capitalist Agriculture. These demises are no more a cause of deep concern.

Sad enough, but serious efforts from all walks of life are to be envisaged to eradicate this misery.

Hopefully, the early sunshine would soon glitter the Golden – Ridges to eradicate such miseries once for all.

Through out history, water even more than land shaped the social behavior of man.

In the recent times, the depleted fresh water reserves and the growing menace of Global Warming—seem to drift the distressed—peasants towards a dead end.

My sincere tributes to Ms. Augusta Goldin for her wonderful scientific writing of the early 1980's

WATER – TOO MUCH, TOO LITTLE, TOO POLLUTED!

Wherein, she has cautioned everyone on the severe need for co-operative water management on a regional, national and international level. Without such careful planning and co-operation, our civilization as we know it can not survive.

As first of things is water,in this era of ecological devastation – we must pay the price of progress by desalination of sea water to quench the thirsty planet. How mean but all the same so true.

The most promising technologies for the desalination of the sea/brakish water are,

+ Distillation
+ Crystallization
+ Reverse Osmosis
+ Electro-dialysis etc.

Of late, looking at the blazing sun, the Solar desalination plants offer a meaningful promise for the production of fresh water.

Though expensive, we hardly have any choice to quench our thirst.

To sum-up, it is more than anything the scarecity of water – that as like the drying of plants –induces the distressed peasants to wind up their lives.

How Sad?

Let us all retaliate this situation by making every drop count.

The Thorny Trail

PART 1

The Thorny Trail!

Be it Mexico or Sudan,

India or Indonesia,

China or Poland

.............the Peasants still have to walk on the thorny trail! (They must now sweat a little more to feed the planet).

Agriculture, in the present millennium is burdened with the menace of 'Global Warming' and the soaring inputs have crippled it further.

This situation is dragging hoards of farmers towards a dead end every day. Judicious efforts to regain agricultural sustainability can alone resolve the issue to a certain extent.

Modern capitalist agriculture is set to prototype the industrial shop floors - with Hi-tech, Bluetooth & Chip controlled Tractors and the factory turned Seeds and Saplings. These mass production gimmicks often drive the marginal farmers into depression, eventually forcing them to quit the race for the lack of power under their hood.

Obviously, - they still must look at the skies to fill their bowl of grain.

Modern agriculture is highly capital intensive and is merciless on the ecological front. The shortcomings, could be summed as under,

1. It essentially focuses on large farm holdings – out riding the marginal peasants, whose only asset is their ability to work in the scorching sun.
2. It breeds hybridization, thus forcing abundant use of inputs and Agro chemicals – while degrading the soil with every harvest.
3. This vicious play often clones toxicity into the food grains - thereby endangering the life on the planet.
4. It is even a riskier business, as the higher capital out lay cannot sustain the havocs of global warming.
5. To achieve optimum productivity, added inputs have to be pumped in –with each sowing- making, soil degradation - inevitable.
6. In modern agriculture - Monoculture & Mechanization go hand in hand & – they both seem to enhance the environmental damage.

The Dream Forbidden

The intentional end of a life or suicide is not merely the end of one's living but a sad defeat of his struggle for living!

The ongoing text is a close resemblance of the tragic demise of a peasant *–Ramu,* who was ultimately torn between living and livelihood.

Onion, the –The pungent purple spicy-tuber grown in the tropics, is an essential ingredient of our daily meals. The aura is so pungent that it leaves eyes watering while being gritted in to fines.

The crop is very labour intensive and capital oriented too! Thus it inherently calls for precise and skilled agronomic practices to reap optimum harvests.

At the same time the **Onion** market is ever trickier – even trickier than the bullion market. The occasional steep upward surges often surf the lucky ones to mingle into bundles of money, for a while - leaving most of the peasants, only to drink and forget it, as a bad joke. A real boon –doggling situation on accord of its short shelf life and odourous handling.

Despite this vicious crop – cycle, – many Peasants are still lured into it – merely in hope of full-filling their dreams within a short span of four months!

Ramu, was one such an enthusiastic pleasant, in his early thirties and though well-built, he was tired of living hand to mouth with traditional rain- fed agricultural cropping pattern.

Annoyed of this 'Money – Less' cycle – he decided to go for cash crops like the ONION.

It needed lot of money for sure!

Subsequently, he drained years of his savings to drill a new bore – well and borrowed some additional sum from the witty private money lender - to pump the water out of the deep well.

Innocently—he wasn't fully aware of the exorbitant rate of interest that laced every drop of water that gushed from the pump to the field to nurse his dream filled *Onion* saplings. Unknowingly he was being entangled into an endless trap of private borrowings. (That seldom spared anyone living)

Four months of hard work in the ravishing sun, coupled with oddly-timed coarse meals - had already sucked the nectar from Ramu's masculine built. It all left him pretty weak and feeble just before the harvest of the shiny purple Onions. The ongoing sickness was however laced with the joy of money that would soon pour into the basket of the toiling family – upon the harvest of these tubers/onions.

Often bad luck precedes on the path of good people and fortune often favours fools!

Who, knew that Ramu's misfortune would soon have only one sad way out – his exit!

The prices of the Onions suddenly shrinked to an all time low, that even the harvest cost was a blow below his belt, leave asides, the packaging, handling and the transportation costs.

What a sinful crop? No wonder why one won't cry while peeling it off!

Lack of storage capacity and the perishability of the crop forced Ramu - to haul the shiny purple ONIONS, to the nearby market where moneyed traders,were used to liquidate the peasants dreams with frozen blood.

How sad – one's profit was someone's burial?

Even this ordeal of hauling the entire harvest to the storage yards of these seasoned traders wasn't a smooth ride for peasants like Ramu – who had limited resources on hand.

Without recourse – Ramu, opted for a rented truck – that quoted exhorbitantly in the wake of few days of waiting in the que for the auction turn at the ONION – market.

The market scenario – with clusters of the eager farmers sporting soiled clothes and with empty stomachs – was no less than a battle field. (It was a routine battle of life for millions of toiling Peasants like Ramu) Sleepless nights, inadequate shelter and stale meals at the market yard – turned the ONION auction yard into an auction yard of the Peasant's lives.

It was the noon of the third summer day when Ramu's turn for the auction was announced. Few minutes later the sales proceeds of his crop made Ramu. literally faint in the annoyed truckers cabin.

The net sales realization on deducting the trade commission, market cess, portal levies etc. fell little short to take care of the annoyed truckers rent.

The clever trucker immediately sensed that Ramu would be unable to square-up his deal. Cunningly, he snatched the entire sum from Ramu's shivering hands and man – handled him with abuses for the short payment – before quitting the pungent smelling market yard, as a bad joke of the day!

The whole trauma left Ramu ever crippled. He hardly had any strength to stand on his own. His throat – dry and head heavier made his heart throb with increased hypertension.

Few minutes later – Ramu's neighbor – Peasant, Dattu, spotted him and rushed for help. The penniless friend was kind enough to fetch a pale of dirty water from the nearby filthy canteen, of the market yard.

The shot of the turbid water of the village canteen took some time for Ramu to regain his senses. However, the mental fatigue still held Ramu from making it to his distant home all by himself.

The sun was already drowning into the horizon to fill darkness into Ramu's shattered eve.

Ramu's Village Badapur- was over two miles from the market yard and with the twilight summing up the day – Dattu, hurriedly tugged his bruised companion on to his back and slowly started making it to Ramu's home – where Sarita – Ramu's only daughter and wife Shaila were anxious to greet him with money in pockets and bulky shopping bags in both of his hands!

Here on the way home – the cold breeze gummed the blood on the Ramu's bruises but the tears in his eyes were getting plentier. What a pity? That too on his very turkey day!

As it started getting darker – Shaila become ever restless with an unusual fear. As she had already expected Ramu to be home by then.

She knew RAMU had to live on the coarse dry food for last few days and it must have been hectic for him. All the same she looked joyous as tonight she would be cooking something sweet for the family – upon Ramu's arrival.

As the darkness started invading – Shaila got tensed up as Sarita started crying aloud for food and for her long promised....*Brand New – Slate !*

The lady of the house smeared off the tears from the child's cheeks and reaffirmed her of a new slate very soon.

She knew how dear Sarita was for Ramu and in any case he would not come home without a new slate for her.

Now, the kerosene lamp in her house was flickering with the cool breeze – mounting her anxiety into a superstitious fear and before she hoped for the better she heard their neighbor Dattu – calling her from their courtyard.

Hurriedly, she opened the door and helped Dattu to make exhausted Ramu rest rather comfortably on the cow – dung plastered floor of their courtyard. Without – breaking the silence – Dattu simply bid Shaila – Good Bye with grief and disappeared in the black of the night.

At first, the soiled clothes and the bruised ankles – gave Ramu, the look of an habitual alcoholic but, as she focused the lamp on to his eyes – the refraction of the tiny tear droplets convinced her that the fate had once again betrayed them.

Shaila – though illiterate; was a courageous lady. She immediately erased the dreams from the slate of her mind and started applying the remaining few drops of kerosene (- cooking - fuel) on Ramu's bruises.

Obviously, - the family went to bed without any food – even on their turkey day.

It was something beyond sadness!! – With the soil stripped off the crop and the crop liquidated – the peasant still slept hungry.

It was perhaps an unusual testimony of grief – where money and struggle never met.

No one knew that this sorrowful night would dawn into yet another sad day for RAMU.

Early in the morning, Ramu greeted the on coming twilight of the dawn, with ever depressed mind & an aching body.

Moments later, he stood up on his aching feet and opened the window. The cool breeze gushed in and started refreshing his sore tissues.

As his sight mapped the horizon – the golden rays of the rising sun cherished a sigh on his lips. The sun rays had magically started energizing his exhausted flora and Ramu soon started recuperating to normal from the trauma of the last night.

To his misfortune, this joyous transformation lasted only for a while until he noticed Shaila – drag Sarita by the collar, towards the village school. The chill swept – Ramu's heart – throbbing, for he knew that, ...

Sarita was refusing to go to school without the promised New slate and was Simply crying aloud for A New Slate

Her yellings faded as she was being dragged closer to the school – However the echoes of their misery started humming exponently in to Ramu's ears.

It wasn't just the matter of a broken slate – but of the broken heart of an innocent father. It was something beyond Imagination.

"The thought of Sarita's broken slate – left Ramu shivering all over – for he had sensed the defeat of his struggle!"

Torn between living livelihood – he now had only one sad option

……. To bid farewell to the. . . . Mother earth!

The postmortem of Ramu's corpse – a few days later, revealed nothing but,

Hunger and Sorrow!

Needlessly,

- ✦ The postmortem of the society we live in,
- ✦ The postmortem of the Political Power we are all latched to & the postmortem of our Religion…… may have quenched the distressed soul.

Furthermore, even if Ramu would have somehow brought a new slate for *Sarita*, his dream for graduating her would still have been a dream alone. This is because of the severe inequality that exists in our education system.

People with marginal income are forced to enroll their pupils into sub standard, overcrowded schools with very poor infrastructure – leaving them-handicapped to compete with the children of rich people—who on the strength of their riches pass out with an upper edge on all fronts.

As a result—many stars in the making are faded before they shine in the field of sports & education.

Consequently—if this inequality is erased, then there would be no distress amidst the toiling peasants nor would they be left stranded on a dead end any more.

As like Ramu – as an adversity stricken farmer – I too was falling prey to the foul play of fate & survival.

The soaring interest on my borrowings for the bore well & the farm machinery soon rendered me hen – pecked and powerless to save my patch of land in the event of crisis.

Suddenly, the thought of Ramu's demise left me spine chilling in the heat of the day. Moments later Sarita's broken slate flashed in my mind and with all the worldly might in to my mind, – I decided not to give up! At – least for Sarita's sake!

With an ever greater confidence from within – I simply glanced around and noted that the – brazilion creeper – which my brother in law Vijay had gifted me few years earlier, was creeping ever higher - embracing the narrowing coconut tree trunk of my farm.

The tip of the creeper was swarming on the flutes of the gentle breeze – making me forget everything – even my existence.

Later, my eyes focused on the root zone of the creeper, only to find that the fines of my fathers ashes had revitalized the soil so rapidly.

Little later, when I had pulled back into reality - the defeat made me uneasy and outraged on my own self, – I started squeezing the stale news paper roll that I was holding for long.

As though heavens had bestowed on me – happiness gushed again all over me and looking at the bruised news paper roll in my fist – I felt to be richest man on the planet. May be even ten times richer than the one time tycoons like the Rockefellers & the Onassis etc.

The old news paper was like Ureka to me. With this Ureka in hand, I knew everything would be all right once again.

"The Butterflies & the Honey bees would soon swarm on the greens of our Peasants and sing a Song of six pence for them "!

(Even I never knew when the piece of paper - later, turned to be the capsule for nursing plants resourcefully !)

CHAPTER 3

Global Warming

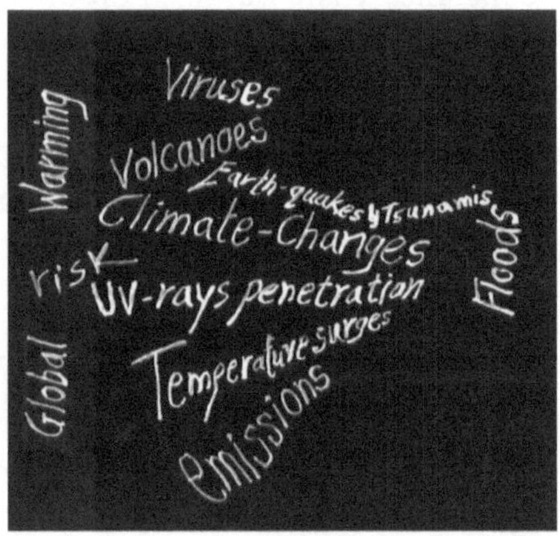

Agriculture & Global Warming

Global Warming ......
A threat more alarming than the Nuclear Warfare!

Mono-culture and Soil compaction
add to Global Warming.

Hazardous chemicals and polluting
machinery, constantly foul the ecology.

Truly – if each one of us plants even a single tree in their entire life – the tree would shield us from the evils of global warming.

How simple a remedy!

It, still – though, seems to be a difficult task!

Agriculture and Global Warming are so closely knit that to me, they seem to be the two facets of a coin.

To understand *Global Warming*– understanding *Agriculture* is very vital –for the perils of *Global Warming* endanger agriculture – the most!

In nut - shell , the operational sequence of agricultural crop production cycle could be narrated as under,

1. Clearing of the field residues of the previously harvested crop, by uprooting the unwanted weeds/ pods manually.

2. Ploughing of the field-subsequently and then allowing it to aerate under the sun for a minimum of one weeks duration (This way the roots and the seeds of the weeds dry up). again allow it to aerate for at least 3-4 days.

3. Subsequently – Raking or criss-cross harrowing is done to disintegrate the crop residues into trash/bio-mulch and also obtain finer tilth of the soil.

4. After another 3-4 days, blade harrow is used to till the soil to finer texture.

5. Depending on the crop – the sowing is done by means of seed cum fertilizer drill.

6. Immediately thereafter the water ways are formed taking into consideration the slope of the land and the topography in general.

7. First watering is done at the earliest (within few hours of sowing).

8. Then after a gap of 2-3 days another quick sip of irrigation water is administered.

9. Most of the seeds thus germinate to cover the soil with a green carpet within 8-10 days of the sowing operation.

10. There after the timely crop nursing operations as under have to be performed,
    i.   Initial de-weeding
    ii. Subsequent fertigation
    iii. Crop protection sprayings
    iv. Raking of the intermittent soil for added aeration and better plant growth.
    v.   Second de weeding and fertigation
    vi. Crop protection spraying if the need be
    vii. Harvesting of the crop
    viii. Threshing/winnoying of the crop for the recovery of the grains.
    ix. Packing and storage for short duration
    x.   Marketing

All the aforesaid operations have to be performed in a particular time frame within the crop's growth cycle.

Further if the nature betrays them – then the Peasants had it!

Above all the market surges account for the final havoc in the agricultural crop production cycle.

Thus the plight of the distressed ones is unimaginable.

Anyway , such a living is all a matter of luck.

A noted spiritual leader late Muktanandswami of the SYDA Foundation, always said that the human life was but. . . .

.........a play of consciousness!

Likewise, I feel that the Agriculture these days is but,

.... a play of *Energy & Labour*.

Obviously, - without the fuel and the power, agriculture would be henpecked and rather worse without the working hands on the fields!

Conventional agriculture in the tropics – calls for turning the soil up side down for at least three or more times upon each harvest – to enable the subsequent plantation be – ever productive !

Now the point is that – is it possible – with the diesel – fuel prices soaring upto Rs. 60/- mark per just a thousand droplets (i.e. 1000ml) ?

IT IS IMPOSSIBLE!

Except for the helpless farmer – everyone is aware of this grim reality. The poor peasant doesn't have the strength to revolt as all of it is drained in feeding the planet. Heredity, perhaps takes its own time for the unrest.

Now, the fact remains – that either the peasants wait for some celestial mercy to be bestowed on them,

OR

......they must move on – carving their way meticulously over the thorny trail.

Carving the way on this trail, is indeed gruesome and may be the Golden – Ridges,

.........with the integration of the Capsule- growing concept would induct some joy in this strenuous occupation of the millions of Peasants.

Agriculture of our times could be redefined as the,

.....*Laborious Craft* of growing,

Food, Feed & Fodder With Faith & Patience Under Several Uncertainities!

...Now the obeyance with Nature, alone would save this age old culture from *Global-Warming* !

Global warming & the Green House effect :

(The phenomenon adversely affects the vast expanses of the perennial – vegetation and the green sinks that boast of life on this planet).

Global warming has sprung up, from the depletion of forests and the ever diminishing Bio – diversity! We have already reached the threshold – where each single tree alone would keep us alive somehow!

Trees and other *Cover- Crops* – breathe in carbon dioxide and release oxygen in turn. It is due to this wonderful gift of the Nature alone – That we could tolerate the ever rising Industrial and Automotive pollutants for so long.

Today, with the ever depleting tree – lines, the harmful emissions tend to saturate the earth's bio-sphere in the form of a thin layer,(like the layer of varnish on the copper wire or the, lacquer - film on the shiny – cricket - ball). Consequently – the sun's rays refracting from the earth's crust in the form of the infra red radiation – get trapped under this shield – thus increasing the temperatures of the earth's crust – thereby warming the globe, that results into *Global Warming* !(Owing to the green house effect).

Automotive and industrial pollutants comprise of hazardous emission like,

✦ CARBON MONOXIDE
✦ NOXUS FUMES, HYDRO-CARBONS &
✦ HYDRO-FLURON RADICALS.

These emissions have tendency to amalgamate with 'O' radical of the atmospheric oxygen (O2),The left over nascent 'O' radical from the atmospheric oxygen again unites with the "Chlorine" radical of the fresh hydro fluron pollutants —thus breaking the OZONE formation chain.

(Other-wise, the 'O' radical would have combined with atmospheric oxygen to form OZONE— thus strengthening the ozone formation chain).

Just as hazardous Auto Emissions are creating road side havoc every day—the Farm machinery like The Tractors, Harvesters, Excavators, Dozers etc are also creating havoc on the fertile farm lands. This coupled with the spraying of new generation agro chemicals every now & then for the plant protection – has worsened the situation beyond endurance. Not only it is affecting agricultural sustainability but also endangering the health of the farming community besides soil compaction.

This issue is equally threatening but being ignored all the while.

The ill maintained farm machinery particularly in the tropics is adding enormously to this disastrous situation.

The only way out would be to accept the minimum Tillage Theory and the shift over to the Traditional Farming like that of the begone days.

In western or the more developed part of the world, owing to the larger farm holdings and higher degree of farm mechanization – some of the - agricultural machines are very powerful with horse powers to the tune of 500 h. p. Obviously – the menace is bound to be alarming.

Further in the tropics with the diminishing horse & the bullock population the farmer has to rely on petrol vehicles like Motor Bikes and pick-up vans to carry out their own & farm worker's - to & fro transportation.

These days there is hardly any farmer who doesn't burn couple of liters of gasoline each day for carrying out his occupation. With the growing population—this number is also on the rise. So to say with agro chemicals and Agri – Machinery —Agriculture & ECOLOGICAL DAMAGE seem to be going hand in hand and ever greater too !

OFF ROAD/MINING MACHINERY –

Dumpers, Excavators & Jumbo Special Duty Machines, also adds considerably to pollution on fields & consequently to Global Warming !

Thus, diminished OZONE cycle makes a room for the UV rays of the sun light to penetrate easily in to the shrinking - protective ozone layer.

Resulting in to the formation of the *Ozone-Hole* !

This is very serious situation as it leads to an atmospheric havoc giving birth to several devastating calamities like,

+ Spontaneous fires in the woods
+ Holocausts
+ Tornadoes&
+ Tsunamis in the oceanic crust.

As such, the famine stricken communities of this year may be destroyed by flood waters – the very next year !

Every single rise in the environmental temperature offspring's with it, several problems for agriculture, viz

+ Scorching of the leaf stomata,
+ Reduction in the soil fauna, ground water and the starving of the living cells contained in the soil fauna.

..........Besides, the melting of the glaciers and the run – off of top– soils into the oceanic floors.

This imbalance often results into tidal deformation and the seismic faults.

The depleting vegetation on the planet often disturbs the natural cycle of the LAND and THE SEA BREEZE, thus fuelling the climatic changes every now and then. With erratic changes in the climate, agricultural productivity is severally endangered.

So to say, if Global warming be the main devil the toiling peasants are truly, the 'devils disciples'.

I am also deeply hurt to remark that the farmers are the greatest ecological devastators – for I have yet to come across a farmer – planting a tree on the community lands – of his own accord. On the other hand – farmers simply turn their back to the tree felling, in the wake of bringing newer lands under cultivation. They simply turn a deaf ear to the environmental damage done by the Dozer / Excavator, in reclaiming the soils.

It is now a high time that a universal law be enforced with strict punishments for the felling of such trees!

Furthermore – based on their land holdings the farmers must be given yearly tree – plantation target to save the planet. It sure – won't be burdensome on them as they are the ones with spades, crowbars & shovels – the vital tools of tree plantation!

'Global – Warming', cannot be dealt merely by ecological restoration but also by the conservation of resources thro' the promotion of Vegetarian diet.

The following lines from the ISKON's well researched book on Vegetarian diet:

'*THE HIGHER TASTE*' ...,

..........would convince the readers to eradicate Global warming – thro' vegetarianism!

According to the information compiled by the U.S.D.A. – over 90 % of all the grains produced in the USA, is for feeding the livestock - COWS, PIGS, DUCKS & CHICKEN – that finally grace the dinner plates.

Obviously, we get back only one pound of flesh from every sixteen pounds of grain.

'Thus is this incredibly wasteful process of using grains to produce meat.'

As it stands now – more than the third's of the harvested acreage from the world is used to feed animals. If all the earths' cultivatable land be used for the production of Vegetarian food – the planet could easily support a human population of around thirty billion.

So to say – each plate of meat would deprive a family of four from food.

As living Cows are of great value to build a healthy society – there is a need for an ever greater worldwide awakening to save the Cow.

It is like saving the GODS!

For us, Cow is next to our mother. Thus laying an embargo on the wasteful process of meat production would be absolutely in line of curbing the global warming effect – by conserving the precious WATER – that is vital in transformation of fresh patches of land into the greens.

To sum up –first the peasants have to be thoroughly educated on the ecological front and compulsion be laid on them for the ecological – restoration. If this mission is truly triggered off then a day would not be far off – when the global warming would simply be washed off like the snow in the rain!

Mother and the Cow

Just as Agriculture is closely related to Global Warming from the ecological point of view—the Automobile too, is closely knitted to Global Warming.

A street polluting Car

F - 1, Racing Pollution

Automotive pollutants attribute for over 60% of all hazardous emissions and an appropriate reference to these emissions that foul the environment, besides the history of automobile - would be worth while to abreast the readers. (If not, for my obsession - for Automobiles & Auto Racing).

Automotive racing also contributes substantially for increasing environmental hazards. The track trials before the countdown and almost negligible restrictions to produce maximum power on the track—add fuel to the fire called-Automotive pollution.

"AUTOMOBILE"

The efforts in the, evolution of the Automobile probably dates back to the Pre- historic era i.e. ever since man learn't that '*THE ROUNDED OBJECT COULD ROLL*'.

Soon the 'wheel' was invented. It was a landmark in the building of the horse drawn carriages. As the times passed THE HORSELESS CARRIAGE was invented & soon came the AUTOMOBILE.

Brief History of Automobile Production :

Automobile: A self propelled passenger vehicle designed to be operated on ordinary roads.

Unlike many other major inventions the idea of the automobile cannot be claimed for an individual.

"Otto Von Guericke" (1602-86) invented an air pump and was probably the first to make Metals Pistons, Cylinders & Connecting rods –the basic components of the Reciprocating engine.

The First Automobile

According to the RAC & the Automobile club De-France, Nicholas Joseph Cugnot of Lorraine—as the constructor of the first true automobile. Cugnot's vehicle was a large, heavy, steam powered tricycle and his model of 1769 was said to have run for 20 minutes, @ 2¼ m.p.h. speed while carrying four people and to have recuperated sufficient steam power to move again after standing for 20 minutes.

Austrian "Siegfried Marcus" did quite a lot improvements over "Otto-Cycle" and did succeed. However, he denied interest in the entire idea of the automobile calling it "A senseless waste of time & effort"

The Age of Steam" (The Steam Era !)

In about 1840, it was clear that the Steam carriages, had little future. They had much to contend with including the auto machinery attitude of the public and the enmity of the horse coach interests which resulted in such penalties–as a charge of pound 2 for passing a tollgate that cost a horse coach only 3s.

The crushing blow was the locomotive act of 1865, which reduced permissible speeds on public roads to 2 M.P.H. within cities and 4 M.P.H. in rurals. The legislation was known as the Red-Flag Act.

The grip of the steam automobile, on the American imagination has been strong ever since the era of the Stanley Brothers (one of whose cars took the world speed record at 127 mph in 1906).

In the early sixties it was estimated that there were still 7000 steam cars in the U.S. and about 1000 of them in running order.

Benz & The Gasoline Car:

Carl Benz was completely dedicated to the proposition that the I.C. Engine would supersede the horse & revolutionize the world's transportation. He persisted in his efforts to build a gasoline fueled vehicle in the face of many obstacles, including lack of money to the point of poverty and the bitter objections of his associates who considered him unbalanced on the subject.

Daimler: Daimler was a gunsmith previously and very intelligent businessman. In 1890, Diamler-Motoren-Gesellschaft, was founded. Two firms Benz & Daimler were merged in 1926, and sold vehicles named Mercedes Benz. (Mercedes was the name of the daughter born in the Daimler family during the merger period)

Early Efforts In The U.S.:

In November 1895, " Chicago Times Harold" race from Chicago to Evanston & return, the distance-54.36 miles and the total running time was 7 Hrs. and 53 Min. and Duryea's did it.

June 1903 – Ford Motors formation, the company produced 1700 cars during the first year of business.

Ford's basic idea – to turn the Automobile from a luxury & a plaything to a dire necessity - clicked.

This not mass production was Ford's contribution to the world. Mass production was an old idea in Ford's time.

Ford's concept of the automobile as a necessity was much more important than the idea of mass production.

Ford also understood something that has defeated hundreds of automobile manufacturers & the thousands of automobile dealers down the year - *SERVICE !*

In the second year of his company's existence, factory trained mechanics were in the field.

Within two decades the American automobile had won the revolution, Henry Ford had begun. The country was on wheels and the manufacturing and the sale of automobile was main production under the U.S.Economy.

Few technical innovations have received as enthusiastic a reception as the motor vehicle. The demand for automobiles was so great that the fledgling industry of the 1890's became big business during the following decade. There was a rapid increase in the number of manufacturing firms; the total number that entered the industry has never been calculated but we do know that 200 domestic makes of car had appeared on the British market by 1913 and 2900 have been identified in the United States, most of them appearing before World War I. Nevertheless demand persistently exceeded the capacity of the industry to produce. This situation enabled manufacturers who were operating on slender capital resources, to acquire cash payment from their dealers, because the dealers were clamoring for Cars.

The Automobile Industry in brief:

The maturing of the industry did not approach the level reached in the United States, where by 1929 there was one automobile for every six people. In other words, the point had been reached at which the entire population of the United States could be transported by Car simultaneously. The volume of highway travel by private automobile cut heavily into the passenger business of American railways and motor truck competition was becoming a serious threat to rail freight traffic.

The United States was counting its automotive output in millions while other countries were still counting theirs in hundreds of thousands. Consequently, although American methods were widely admired and imitated, they could not be adopted in full. It was simply not economically feasible for European manufacturers to employ the elaborately specialized and highly expensive machine tools that American automobile factories used. Even in as comparatively large scale a producer as Morris Motors, the moving assembly line was not introduced until 1934.

The Darker Side : 'Automobile Exhaust'

Normal Automobile /IC Engine pollutants are Carbon Monoxide Co, Carbon Dioxide CO_2, Sulphur Dioxide SO2 ,Lead &other Noxious fumes,Carbon soot etc.

Devices incorporated into modern automobiles to reduce the above hazardous emissions *(Leave asides the multifolds increase in the population of automobiles itself)* - There are still no efforts taken to check the growing vehicle population.

- ✦ *CARBON CANNISTERS*
- ✦ *POSITIVE CRANK CASE VENTILATION*
- ✦ *MODIFIED ENGINE BREATHERS*
- ✦ *ELECTRONICS IGNITION*
- ✦ *CATALYTIC CONVERTERS/AFTER BURNERS.*
- ✦ *HIGHER COMPRESSION RATIOS & DIRECT INJECTION*
- ✦ *ADOPTION TO CLEANER FUEL BLENDS*

etc. etc. — only to name a few.

To sum-up, that **while living with automotive emissions,** a time is not far off when we will have to……

BURY THE ENGINES,

BEFORE THEY BURY US !

– an anonymous ecologist.

I still remember of having read an artist's perception on the cars of future, in one of the - Time Magazine issues of late 1960's, that

I wish some day, the cars would run on bottled air pollution!

Obviously he hinted on the growing menace of automotive pollution.

Over the decades the Automobile became a dire necessity – the world over, with factories turning out couple of cars every second, (Needlessly fouling the environment with hazardous emissions, every second !)

Somehow—a time has come to give a serious thought to the perils of Automotive emissions or else global-warming would be like a free lancer to plunge into our lives without any pre intimation.

Automotive industry, the term usually applied principally to the manufacture of motor vehicles, although it also includes the manufacture of engine and body parts for motor vehicles. While the automobile is of European origin, the industry became heavily concentrated in the United States.

The impact of Automobile in the world economy is so predominant that without it – the economy of several countries would collapse overnight.

From 1955 to 1960 for example, world automobile production approximated 12000000 vehicles annually of which between 60% and 65% were made in the U.S. The economic importance of the industry was so greet that automobile output became the principle index of U.S. business conditions and of one of the important elements in the economic recovery of Western Europe. After World War II, was the marked expansion of motor vehicle production.

Along with the manufacture and sale of motor vehicles and parts the automotive industry brought into existence a substantial group of enterprises engaging in service functions. The scope of these can be indicated only briefly. In the early 1960s the United States alone had about 188000 gasoline service stations, 74000 independent repair shops and 23000 dealers in automotive accessories. Great Britain had 5000 service stations and 12500 firms engaged in repair work and the sale of fuel and accessories.

Stock Car - Speed Racing

Stock Car - Scramble

Agriculture & Banking!

Another young farmer comes along – who wants to buy it, but hasn't got the money to pay for it !

"The die – hard demise of Ramu should be an eye opener to reform Agriculture on all fronts – including Agricultural Banking"

What a life – taking play of numbers, was incorporated by the private money lenders in mid 19th century !

102	104/04	106/12
108/20	110/40	112/61
114/84	117/16	119/50
121/89	124/33	126/82

➤ A back breaking equation of the 1950's on the thorny trail of private borrowings!

Rs. 100/- received upon deep humiliations after the day long wait, on the eve of the 1st day of the month

– wickedly matured into Rs. 127/- in the mere lapse of twelve months!

(Dragging the peasant towards a dead end)

Regretfully for ordinary farmers, agricultural banking is still the same even in this millennium,

✦ *Piles of Papers,—*for handful of money!

OR

✦ *More of thumb impression, & less of dimes!*

Bitter banking experiences of the marginal peasants have rendered agricultural banking from a mere play of numbers to a bad joke of emotions!

How SAD?

The renowned statesman Sir, George Bernard Shaw, once sarcastically made a mention of the banker as to be a;

"Person who lends you an Umbrella when the sun shines & snatches it away when it Starts raining!"

With my years of unpleasant banking experiences – I could sense the truth in the lord's witty observation.

In agriculture – the crop production cycle has to advent through innumerable uncertainties, viz

1. The barometric and the temperature surges
2. The storm and the viruses, besides spurious – seeds, chemicals and fertilizers etc.

As such; unlike the industrial sector – the repayment of agricultural borrowings can not be precisely predicted. In this dependable situation, the peasant is forced to loose credit worthiness almost with each harvest.

This unhealthy scenario induces the bankers to snatch the umbrella from him in the rainy season.

Thus, trapped in the painful cycle of interest, the market levies, the trade brokerage and the handling of agricultural produce – the Peasants often get dragged towards a dead end.

I strongly feel that, any venture circumscribed with several uncertainties, can not be fruitful on borrowed capital. May be the good – old barter – trade in exchange of commodities, could hold good in these times—shadowed with global warming.

Truly speaking, Peasants must learn to conserve further and also think twice before making any purchases and try to carry out their occupation with minimal borrowing – as, then alone few dimes would slip into their pockets.

The interest has only exponential growth and is always ruining.

Interest is like the cancer cell that seldom spares, anything living. Just as wise men reform their lifestyle to keep such killer instinct away – the peasants must also keep borrowings at a hands distance.

History reveals that *INTEREST* has killed countless Peasants – let each demise serve as a cursor to alarm the young dreamy enthusiasts in agriculture.

As a child, I was awestruck, when my father's best friend had to loose his land in the wake of small private borrowings.

The money lenders would never let the borrower sleep and the borrower would hardly stand on his feet if he repaid the borrowings in one stroke. It was like the one way traffic with the very road leading to a dead end.

Soon after Independence in 1947, – the banks took over the money lending business and hope seem to percolate in the lives of the weaker farming section.

Today these banks have fattened into the megacrops – by primarily serving the industrial sector. Though the things have changed a little for better,the darkness of the interest still haunt the peasants like their own shadow.

Sometimes – jokingly, I feel that some one from the financial sector with a social angle should soon start a *"Good Night Banking Corpn"*(A Global – Bank with a life saving mission)

….That would charge interest to the borrower on his working hours only – so that the borrower – at least sleeps peacefully at night. (How illogical – man works for around eight hours but has to pay interest on borrowings for twenty four hours).

I AM OBVIOUSLY HINTING AT REDUCING THE INTEREST BURDON OF EVERY BORROWER TO A THIRD!

Sad enough, despite the bank's growing infrastructure to serve the rural hubs – private money lending practices can not be eradicated. They still have their own stakes &significance worldwide,

Instant Money for Blood !

Despite imposition of several restrictions on private money lenders – the illiterate peasants still have to raise few thousands by keeping his beloved wife's necklace (Mangal Sutra) with the money lender. Thus the wife's necklace that is usually taken off only at the funeral rites of the Peasant's beloved – is now forced to serve as an ATM for him, what a plight of the distressed son of the soil?

Such situation arises only because the MEGA-CORPS (The corporate Banks) still hesitate to serve the rural folks perhaps for the lack of business quantum. They prefer lending huge sums to few giant industrial establishments – while delivering flowery talks of socio – economic upliftment on the well decorated stages, every now and then.

Agricultural borrowings – cannot be precisely monitored and the arrears / defaults, are largely attributed to the,

✦ High interest rates,
✦ Higher service charges & levies

(Like mortgages, processing fees and the subsequent compounding of the interest).

Last but not the least is……

The delay in disbursements and the inadequate sanctions etc.

All these unfortunate conditions simply drift the borrower into depression even prior to the disbursements of his loan. Obviously, - the depressed soul is unable to produce optimum yields and often gets swayed from an healthier life to erratic living.

Borrowings and the Defaults are respectively the circumference and the radius of the vicious circle of LOAN.

In olden days – when there were no banks – at times of crisis the Peasants had to knock the doors of the money lenders. The god fearing farming community often condemned those farmers who fell for this option. As such there was a moral binding on the borrowings in general. So to say, only ten out of hundred fell prey to this cancerous interest trap. In the event of failure of the crop on account of some natural circumstances few – borrowers had to give up their pledged lands to square up the principal sum and the compounded interest.

It was a profound tragedy that often cloned with it – the peasants next few generations!

Today in the wake of modernization of agriculture – queues of farmers are seen spiraling, the bank premises – leaving the fields helpless without the working hands.

Borrowing is no more humiliating as it used to be in the olden days. In fact it is now becoming – a status symbol to flank credit cards every now and then. Thus with this extravagant life style, out of every hundred borrowers at least sixty odds, get into the banks red ledgers. This is only for the lack of moral binding on the borrowings.

I am not an economist but an interest – laden, Peasant and so I feel it worth while to caution the young toilers – not to make any offering to the mother earth on borrowed money. The mother is always the mother – who knows only to give without any expectations.

Let us not trade her for our living but sincerely worship her by sweating a little more each day.

Remember, the mother would never let us down – as it blossoms even richer with our last remains – the funeral ashes !

I don't intend to blame the bankers either as they are forced to perform like a cluster of money lenders. No one looks at the Peasant's loan proposal in Toto. Everyone reviews it from his own angle – safeguarding his own territory there by delaying/denying the whole affair.

Bankers often enjoy the best work environment and their only deity is THE – MONEY. They breathe in the air full of commerce every now and then – so emotions have no room in their SAFES and VAULTS. They simply do not reckon to what the delivery of the daughter in pain – means to the family of the distressed.

Even in the event of a small default their recovery men simply force the hen pecked borrower to meet the manager in the A.C. cabin – Prior to escorting the lady in pain to the maternity home.

Once for all, the peasants must be very careful before making any borrowings. They must always remember that every dime that spins out of the safes of the bankers or the money lenders is fouled with the interest before it springs up into his palms.

Just like the fouled seeds fail to germinate – the interest laden capital (with borrower under stress) seldom blossoms into a wholesome harvest.

Borrowings leads one to sleeplessness, frustration and depression. At times it results into,

- ✦ Emptying of grains from the SILOS,
- ✦ Shovels from yards,
- ✦ Jewels from the dear ones,
- … Thus drifting the joy from life!

So think ten and one times before holding the loan disbursement token in the hand.

Actually,Agriculture is an occupation of the millions of Peasants and so there ought to be Banks to serve this sector on exclusive basis may be this could be made possible with the formation of--

"THE KISAN FINANCE CORPN."

These corporations should also serve as the nodal agency by rendering remunerative services on various trades of agriculture with the state of art techno – feasibility reports, training of rural man power and providing market information and access to infrastructure. These agencies would also monitor the project during its moratorium period.

As the Agriculture would be their main play arena – they would have their own regional farms with principle crops of the region cultivated on those farms. This way they could get closer to the plights of the borrower. The newer technique's on these farms would induct greater confidence into the borrowers.

Furthermore – in order to minimize the n.p.a in the agriculture sector, the banks must train and hire the rural unemployed youth to perform as their official commercial agents to conduct daily auction of the agricultural commodities on their behalf in the market yard. These agents would have the list of their borrowers, who would be bound to auction their produce through these agents only.

The agents would not charge any trade brokerage from these members and would make a compulsory E

– Recovery of min 20 % of the sales proceeds without recourse and furnish him with the receipt of the said transaction on the spot.

In this manner there would be frequent direct recoveries from the borrower upon the sales of their several agriculture products like vegetables, milk, eggs, cereals, fodder, fruits, poultry and fish etc. thus helping him regain his – credibility.

The banks in turn would benefit from the timely recovery and the additional large volumes of Cash flow in to their safes every day.

The on-line E – recovery, would also save the borrower from depositing small laugh worthy sum, physically into his loan quantum and protect his account from becoming an npa.

For ex. if the peasant brings say only one 20kg crate of tomatoes to the market and its sales proceeds be approximates Rs. 300/- then Rs. 60/- would be E – transferred to his crop loan account automatically.

However without such transfer mode—he would be humiliated to deposit such a meager sum physically in to his account.

For ex. if the peasant brings say only one 20kg crate
of tomatoes to the market and its sales proceeds be
approximates Rs. 300/- then Rs. 60/- would be E –
transferred to his crop loan account automatically.

However without such transfer mode—he would be
humiliated to deposit such a meager sum physically in to
his account.

Lastly about SUBSIDY on farm inputs, it often lures the farmers to buy things only because for sake of the SUBSIDY. The subsidy norms further push them into the loan cycle thus making things miserable once for all. So the purchases must be absolutely need based irrespective of subsidy.

To sum-up, the peasants must restrict the borrowing only to their emergencies. They must honor their occupation and learn to be content. They must as far as possible perform their occupation in harmony with nature by adopting following methodology. (Which probably their ancestors adhered to)

- ✦ Can we not carry out farming without very high – tec mechanization?
- ✦ Can we not prepare our own – manure, thro' appropriate waste recycling?
- ✦ Can we not reap harvest – without the combines?
- ✦ Can we not conserve water without control irrigation i.e. by adopting contour irrigation, elimination of leakages & subsoil mulching techniques etc. and may be-the shift over to capsule growing over the golden ridges.

YES WE CAN! – (*Only by sweating a little more each day*)!

Hopefully, agricultural banking must serve to be a **tool to prosperity** and not as the **toll to adversity**!

The Indian mythology – has defined the toiling Peasant as the "BALI - RAJA".

....Signifying that he is someone lion hearted,with the strength of a bull in the biceps.

Further, RAJA or the KING is someone who showers wealth and riches on the dearer and deserving ones. So let us all peasants work little harder to bring back the lost kingly glory to our occupation – instead of pledging to Banks – every now and then.

With years of toil and sweat – the day would not be far off when the only reason the Peasant walks into the Bank is for depositing the money and not for borrowing it.

Nothing is really impossible; for

+ Farming was in top – gear in the Indus valley during the Harappan civilization period.
+ The Nile basin was transporting ship loads of long staple Egyptian – cotton to various continents even when there were no BT seeds or the mechanical combines.

Agriculture in those days must have had the will to drive on! Let us retrieve history to bring back the golden era in our lives.

Lastly the farmers also should avoid diversion of funds as it is like robbing ones mother. It not only creates problem for the bank but also eventually ruins the borrower.

Also the banks must adopt some farm to study the economics of various crops and their payback etc. This would bridge the gap between lending & borrowings. Several situations like untimely finance and inadequate finance would be self explanatory in such system. Effects of Global Warming would also be a rationally linked in rescheduling the loans or the interests thereon.

Lastly—it would transform the Banker into a Farmer and bring joy into this occupation.

CHAPTER 5

Caution: This road leads to a dead end

+ Soaring Agricultural inputs,
+ Scanty Rainfall and shortage of man power,
+ Dearer fuel/ energy costs &,
+ The ever fluctuating prices of commodities,

.....have crippled modern Agriculture, beyond recuperation.

To focus on the altruism – the average peasants are even unable to make it daily to their remotely located farms with fuel for his bike – escalating to Rs. 70/- per 1000 droplets. Obviously, with hardly any one to manage the show on the field – one could very well imagine the fate of the Agricultural productivity!

Even if he determines to make daily visit to his farms – he must blend gasoline in his bike with 40% cheapper kerosene fuel. What a tragedy? Leave apart the smoke and the jerks of the detonating mixture.

Blending of gasoline with Kerosene, not only induces the guilt of violating the pollution norms (on accord of excessive smoke emissions) but also subjects them to constant street abuses by the, smoke – annoyed , white collard motorists who don't have a slightest idea of the Peasant's struggle for living !

This economic run down compels us to- peep into the peasant's – ancestor's life and research as to how they carried out occupation in older times.

✦ With no Public transportation,
✦ Poor communication
✦ Limited resources and
✦ The lack of infrastructure etc.

Whatever the odds be – they were true to their occupation.

They worshipped nature – produced healthy food and had deep concern for the ruminants and the soil fertility.

As such, today's younger generation in agriculture must minutely – explore & analyze, as to . . . .

+ What was their daily routine?

+ What was their life – style and food habits?

+ How was their marketing etc.(minimum risk)?

Whatever it be – they boasted of a

+ Strong Physique & A Strong Will

These abilities helped them surf thro' all the odds in their life.

We must also stretch our reins in time or else we too would be washed away like the run – off soils upon a heavy downpour, into the oceanic floors.

Let us staunchly face the evils of Global warming and not just kneel down to its threats.

No matter how – rough the road – lacing it with trees and greens alone would help us overcome this unhealthy situation.

Let me recollect the faint memories of my school days at the Sainik School, Satara – having come across a very touching novel on the agony of Agriculture,

'THE GOOD EARTH'

–By Pearl S Buck

The book focused on the post war sorrows of the female bonded farm labourers in china. The mothers were forced to administer a shot of opium to their infants to make them asleep for long hours – enabling them slog for the whole day on the community farm for their bowl of grain.

Those days – I thought that the book was a mere piece of fiction but as I grew up, I learnt that adversity had only changed its facet over the period of time.

Today – with no Opium at hand, the cries of the little ones - simply get diffused in their drying throat while their mothers are getting tarnished in the harshness of the sun on the fields.

As I stepped up from the school to the college – I found my father to be rather serious, most of the times. Perhaps the exhaustive field work must have toned him that way.

All the same – his tuning with nature all the while – matured him to be full of wisdom though schooling was a mere pipe – dream for him – all his life!

With my close association of over three decades with him – he never spoke of MONEY – as it was still a dearer commodity for him. The wrinkles on his forehead, hinted me of the humiliations that he had to go through all his life, for the sake of education. He always felt ashamed to be illiterate but somehow he managed to scribble his name to avoid thumb—impressions. This is how he managed to hide his illiteracy.

Illiteracy made him tough for the times and I had to abide by him, despite of my higher education and the business experience.

'ILLETERACY & EDUCATION'

They aren't that apart – as generally thought to be!

In fact illiteracy has its own upper edge and often proves to be a boon in disguise. It compels one to obey the laws of nature rather religiously. Obviously – the illiterate

46

peasants live a healthy life in their open to sky class room where nature is the sole teacher of every subject. These Peasants often pass on the baton of this natural life cycle on to their next generation. The nature in turn teaches them to be realistic – though, depriving them from the contemporary system of education. But even then, their learning doesn't stop. Their mud paved hut ments seem to transform into the temples of wisdom,with nature as the custodian and their parents as the trustees.

Their parents, who had come a hard way – always caution their children on the godly curses and the fury of the nature – if they ever tried to trade their morals in life with evils and vices. They constantly alarm their little ones on the,

- *FEAR OF MONEY*
- *FEAR OF SOCIETY AND THE,*
- *FEAR OF DARKNESS IN LIFE!*

This FEAR compels the little ones to live a bonded life with a limited vision. Like a tree with restricted root – zone always makes its way – up all the while. This is how they groom up to be the worthy citizen of the nation.

Thus having forced to live a consolidated life – they seem to take care of their health and be content even while the clouds of poverty are darkening on them.

It is perhaps for these fearful teachings of life – my father always seemed to be contented.

At times – I feel agriculture to be the best tutor. Just like the seeds must be conditioned prior to sowing – the grooming Peasants in the making, take on life by observing the seeds mature into a sapling in the heat of the day and the chill of the night.

Though the seed treatment helps the seed to survive – it still has to germinate by itself.

Obviously, it is always the metal within that at counts!

A well educated man may become a statesman – but the illiterate peasant who cultivates the young saplings to blossom into a rich harvest is full of environmental wisdom! Let us honor his devotion and integrity with the nature without any recourse.

The peasants in villages, producing food for the planet seem to have inherited contentment and peace of mind from their ancestors – while walking on the thorny – trail.

Today with the environment – fouled and the soil endangered – the obeyance with nature and the blessing of our forefathers would alone bring a ray of hope into our depressed lives.

Now coming to the plight of the millions of landless farm – laborers, their agony is worser, as all their roads seem to terminate to a dead end.

They are in the *RACE OF LIFE* as long as there is juice in their balls. (Pardon me for being ever realistic) Once – they are drained out it they really had it!

What a pity?

With,. . .

✦ No Provident Fund or Gratuity

✦ No Pension or Insurance

✦ No Medicare or Rather No Life !

They can't even buy a bottle of Benadryl (A common cough syrup) leave alone – treating of serious illnesses, like hypertension, renal failure or the cardiac arrests.

The only affordable medicine at hand for these distressed men is perhaps a shot of country – liquor to drift from their exhaustive day into few dreams laden hours to the dawn.

The farm labours are the backbone of agriculture and it would be a sin to ignore them. Moreover their welfare would prevent deforestation – at it is the only side income for them (Selling of fuel wood).

The growing monoculture and the crop oriented farming culture are other evils of modern agriculture

For Examples.

........Several thousands of acres of grape vineyards in Australia,

.... lacs of acreage under sugarcane in India, Brazil, Cuba and the West Indies as also

.........vast plains under wheat in Central America and northern India

...etc only to name a few.

Besides soil erosion – these mass production crop belts have already – driven the Sparrows and the Butter flies, far away – endangering the ecology of the terrain.

Furthermore the robotic operations that precede with mono culture often hamper the health of the cultivators with the induction of disorders like

+ Spondylitis
+ Bronchitis
+ Viruses, piles, hypertension, cancer etc

... On account of Tractamount sprayers cum mist blowers, systemic agrochemicals and pollution due to mechanization.

Secondly, the awesome rat – race amidst various monoculture societies leads to egoistic rivalry and is unhealthy for the farming community in general. For ex. at home – the grape growing cluster think themselves to be the most progressive agriculturists in the country while the Pomegranate cluster now thinks that they could take the Grape growers for a ride any time.

This rivalry induces selfishness into these cultivars creating an unhealthy productivity barrier between the Tiny Peasants and the Land Lords.

Eventually – the SHIFT TO BIO – DIVERSITY ON WHAT – EVER SCALE IS THE NEED OF THE HOUR!

The Golden Ridge to Prosperity – the resourceful bio – diversity farming module has the – strength to curb the monoculture practices.

As agriculture is of global concern,it's fate touches – even those treading on different walks of life. So to say, -no one can neglect agriculture as no one prefers to be HUNGRY!

Agriculture – worldwide is always under debate – as the world's economy circles around it.

Several groups of agronomy – Scholars, Social workers, Researchers, Policy makers, Politicians&Bankers etc. often think about agriculture on different wave lengths.

For ex.

✦ The Researchers – from production angle,

✦ Ecologists from environment angle,

✦ Policy makers from budgetary angle,

✦ Bankers from the recovery angle,

✦ Media from the publicity angle,

✦ Politicians from the voting angle,

✦ Merchants from the trading angle and

✦ The Peasants from the critics angle.

However – there must be someone to think of agriculture from the SARITA'S angle !

As every one's school of thought spins around their own axis, they fail to render proper direction to Agriculture. As such the peasants constantly feel neglected from the main stream.

So – agriculture ought to be deeply explored with grass – root level feed backs.

Mere text and presentations – simply rob the precious time from the peasants – who would otherwise be working on their fields.

In order to achieve Global competency for our Peasants, the agricultural infrastructure be reshaped and strengthened on the need base criteria.

Viz. by establishing,

✦ Innumerable micro cold storages, energized by mere, 3-5 H.P. HI-TEC rotary compressors with solar back-up.

✦ Small rickshaws with handling capacity of 500 to 750 kgs be converted into refer vans to prevent food wastages.

✦ Horticultural pruning wastes and other dry Bio-mass should be shredded to generate cheap electricity by fueling the Gasifiers.

✦ Several small capacity(10 to 020 M.T.) SILOS be made compulsory for every 100 Acres to prevent grain wastages

✦ Clearing forwarding and certification agencies be created at tehsil levels to trigger off exports(These suggestions are only to name a few)

To sum-up, the agriculture worldwide is a tricky affair, as always,

✦ Somewhere there is drought,

✦ Somewhere the floods,

✦ Somewhere the fire,

✦ Somewhere the strikes,

✦ Somewhere the snow – storms and cyclones,

✦ Somewhere the Hurricanes,

✦ Somewhere the ozone holes &

✦ Somewhere the Hard Pans etc.

....Swinging The Pendulum Of Agricultre From Success To Failure

Or

From A Smile On The Lips To Tears In The Eyes!

It is perhaps why – with more than 65 yrs of Independence at home things haven't changed in the proportion for the Peasants. He is still using foot – wares glued with scrapped tractor tyre soles!

- ✦ The good old plough purchased by the father is still being anchored on the backs of the malnourished pair of bullocks. (bred on hybrid – filler grains)- Thus exhausted,they soon have to give up tilling the hard soil pans layered with fouled/polluted air.

This situation is also dragging these unfortunate ruminants to a dead end – every day! Without ruminants organic farming would always remain a mere dream.

Already the wax proto – type of the OX (Bullock) are an item of historical display in the art galleries of Western countries. What a pity? For the godly gender of agriculture!

With growing mechanization – the rift between the peasants and the nature is on the rise. It would ultimately endanger the environment and the ecology.

The Golden Ridge – bio diversity farming is yet another HOPE – though!

CHAPTER 6

The Agony–
(The Grim Reality)

Be it poverty,

or

Natural Disasters,

. . . the Peasants have to sweat a little more to live with it !

No matter – what the agricultural growth indices boast of – prosperity on the fields is still a distant dream as long as the...........

✦ Destitute women farm labourers still have to anchor to the wooden hoe to till the slopey lands.

✦ The young – girls in puberty must crank the crude – oil engines – to spin the flour mills for their bread.

✦ The village lady in pain must make it to the distant maternity home on a rattling bicycle as pillion rider!

My aunt, 'Chandrabhaga' - was only an example of the early 20th century .

(Every such a lady in her times had to go thro' such anagony !...)

Surprisingly,

No one truly revolts against fate! May be that's why the mother earth always fills warmth into the distressed ones. This perhaps is the living cause and the testimony of traditional farming.

These endless sorrows make me mention of my aunt,

CHANDRABHAGA (Named after a sacred Indian river) who passed away at an wholesome age of 92 yrs.

Paralytic for the last two decades – she had lost her father when she was barely six years old & had no brother too (she lost her husband when she was barely 30 years old)!

Customarily her mother Anusayabai, who had only four daughters – married off the eldest – *CHANDRABHAGA* at an early age of fifteen.

Years of hard work in the fields after the marriage, gradually groomed her into womanhood to become a mother of a son at the age of 23.

She named her only son as RAMRAO. With the arrival of Ramrao – the trouble some days seem to have started setting when a severe calamity struck on her.

Her husband died of a short – illness (The epidemic of Plague) leaving her to be a destitute widow at a youthful age of 30. From then on – it was over half a century of mere bull work alone from dawn to dusk for this iron lady.

Agriculture – in those times was going thro' a crucial patch and fund raising in the crisis often compelled the helpless peasants to knock the doors of the wealthy money lenders.

Chandrabhaga was illiterate but she very well knew what private borrowings meant to be. She determinantely started living within her means.

With an iron will – she started dragging the plough of their family to till across the thorny trail. Laborious field harshness of more than twelve hours a day for several decades and that to without a single Sunday – wasn't a joke for Chandrabhaga? Apart from ploughing the fields and sowing them in time – the transformation of the green stems into the golden grain laden straws was yet another painful journey that often froze the peasants sweat into the stomata's of their skin. Thus making them weared, tarnished and old – prematurely.

Further – the harvesting of the crop in the mid-summer and the transportation of the bundles of hope (grain laden golden hay) over the shoulders to the threshing or the winnowing yard – was equally tiresome.

While winnowing, the dew smeared eyes of the peasants hopefully counted every grain bead - drop into the gunny bag while their minds eagerly guessing as to what portion of the harvest would be ground to their bread upon setting off for the borrowings on the crop and the land.

It may appear to be a fictitious script but not for my aunt, who must have slept empty stomach on several of her turkey days.

These reflections, made deep impact on my mind despite the worldly comfort and freedom my father had bestowed on me.

Like the end of a stormy day – things settled down for my aunt only when she was in the early 70's. I still remember the smile on her face when her grandson graduated to be a Chartered Accountant.

At that moment – she seemed to have forgotten the decades of pain and humiliations – as though she had never lived with them.

Her life often reminds me of the veteran actress – late NARGISJI DUTT who portrayed, the destitute woman like Chandrabhaga of rural India in the early 1950's – in Mehboob Khan's all time epical saga on the celluloid. *THE MOTHER INDIA*.

My sincere tributes to Mehboob khan's entire production team – to take viewers so close into the life of the rural folks of the 50's. I wish I could paste a CD of this movie on every book to give a realistic go for the readers on my attempt to eradicate the misery of the *BROKEN SLATE!*

Peasants and their Bollywood Connection:

In this text – I also intend to rope in the '**mannat – makers**' of Bollywood, Hollywood, the Auto and the Industrial magnets, who could merely by scarifying one of their evening meals - bless someone like Ramu for all his life.

In fact the young peasants and the farm labourers are amongst the craziest fans of the celluloid world. They are the true Box office makers, for sitting on the front benches they joyously whistle even on the silliest jokes on the screen.

Agriculture has always provided a strong base for the film makers ever since the veteran film maker "Dadasaheb Phalke" switched on the studio lights for the first time.

Let us now establish a new bond of fraternity amidst the two valuable sects of life,

The Celluoid Entetainers &

The crazy village moviegoers!

For decades together – Cinema has been the sole affordable form of entertainment in the tiresome lives of the Peasants. Cinema – has been embedded so deep into their lives that they visit the nearby Cinema talkie more often than the adjoing – temples, mosques or the churches.

Late, Nargisji Dutt - In the film MOTHER INDIA.

Filmstar, Manoj Kumar as Bharat,
In the Patriotic film UPKAR!

Movies must have been like the cell – phone chargers to them – lacing their dreams with ever brighter colors.

The DONS of the celluloid world may not be aware that these crazy movie goers. With money just enough to buy them the front row tickets – they often cycled for more than 20kms in the darkness of the evening – to slip into their heavenly world of dreams for a few hours.

The simple and innocent lives of these village folks lured several movie makers at homes to create all time master pieces like the,

+ *GODAN*

+ *DO BIGHA ZAMEEN, NISHANT,*

+ *GANGA JAMNA, NAYA DAUR,*

+ *UPKAR, MOTHER INDIA ETC*

So in ways – the movie barons – indirectly owe a lot to the community that grows food for the planet – for their addiction to cinema.

Thus, show – biz world could retaliate the thanks giving by adopting few distressed families and help them with appropriate interest free friendly loan – that would be soon repaid in kinds of health foods, cereals, pickles, fruits and sweets.

Such a gesture would help orphans like SARITA to mature with dignity and be at strides with the girl of the new – era – the professional with a *LAPTOP* in the hand.

These joyous moments would fill warmth and happiness in the life of lonesome film stars who must live only to glitter in the celluloid world.

To the Industrialists – I would request them to pull out their heads from the Wall Street journal for a while and roll back the windows of their limos to feel the fresh air resonating the echo's of SARITA'S broken slate into their ears.

We all know that these gems have the strength to buy a million slates. Let such a noble act cherish Ramu's dream to gift SARITA – a new slate in time!

To sum-up, the show – biz galaxy and the industrial magnets – instead of buying tricky, unknown, urban lands at fortune shelling prices – create new heavens for them, by mending the broken family.

As the show biz world is very mature - having a flair for social work – I earnestly bow to all of them to eradicate miseries like Ramu's brake down from the face of earth once for all.

Obviously – if Ramu would have had even one star brother – he would be yet alive to see SARITA- Walk smilingly into the class with a new – slate! Indeed what an illusionary joyous occasion!

GOD BLESSETH THOSE WHO TRADE THEIR PRESENT FOR THE SORROWS OF THE DISTRESSED!!!!!!

PART 2

The Hope

(Hope is like a small flickering lamp that tries to keep itself ablazed in the ushering winds)

Hope – is like the Miraj in the desert—that keeps the nomads - trailing on and on without water.

Hope – has driven the wheel of Agriculture for ages together.

Hope – has been a mystical factor in the lives of millions of toiling Peasants.

HOPE has kept the wheel of agriculture spinning on and on!

(It has been the only survival key for the millions of toiling peasants.)

I do remember my father holding my hand for a few moments before his death _ with his eyes full of HOPE!

HOPE was all that, I strongly inherited from him. I had to do something to satisfy his soul by making agriculture ever joyous for ever – for I knew of the thorny trail he trailed all his life!

I had lots of constraints – the grafted eyes, pigeon chest, clicking knees, growing hyper tension and the ageing factor.

So what?

All put together – they were still no way closer to Ramu's sorrows or even the life long wrinkles on my father's forehead.

All of a sudden I was full of energy, like a young man with vigor and before, I even sensed of what was happening within,I was already on my way to the farm.

This time I was with a mission. It was not an ordinary farm anymore but it was,

"The Nature Station"….. Laced with corridors of the golden ridges – that held the promises of a new slate for SARITA!

Necessity is the mother of invention:

In recent times, the foaming of agriculture with innumerous ever complicated theories has totally confused the farmer in distress. Also as adversity happens to be the best teacher, many helpless Peasants are being recently attracted towards ,

'ZERO BUDGET AGRICULTURE'

It is a well thought doctrine with a strong & sacred mythological base **'THE COW'**!

If religiously followed—one desi cow can manure over 30 acres of farmland with simple derivatives prepared out of the cow's dung &urinage. The process is simple and the application universal.

What is needed is the drive to accept this age old field proven reality of Heritage farming.

It is a one stop solution to several agricultural problems. Moreover the yields are non toxic and healthier. They have added shelf life and a pleasant aura.

The 'shift- over' would improve soil fauna in a very short period. It is miracular and affordable and in line with *'Save the Cow'* –mission. It is a total cure and an ideal ecological restorer.

In fact *'JEEVAMRUT'* the nectar of zero budget farming is the key to health food production. It's an inevitable tool for the peasants stranded on the dead end !

It is but the life divine!

It imparts total content to farming occupation, besides prosperity.

So let the **'desi cow'**be our main battle tank to combat global warming. Let there be one cow for every hundred freshly planted trees and we are sure to win the war against global warming!

Cow is so sacred that even the goods fear the cow. Let us all worship her for our survival.

The New – Era of Ecological Restoration!

VrukshavalliAmhaSoyariVanchare

'Let us create as many Green-Sinks as the Amazonian or the Iwokrama reserves to bring home the Bees & the Butterflies !'

Ecological restoration would merely remain as a pipe dream as long as peasants in distress are compelled to cut age old trees standing tall on the boundaries of their farms overnight, to pay off their weekly labour payments.

It is not a trifle issue to be just overlooked. If one probes deep into the scenario—the peasants hardly get the 1/3rd of the wood value for what the saw-miller's make out of the fines of the said wood upon this ecological massacre.

In fact it is a racket where the saw mill owners fund the wood suppliers (Woodcutting Contractors) who in turn often remit advances to helpless farmers for uprooting trees from their lands once for all – may be at their convenience.

This vicious circle would never favor ecological restoration even if all of us plant a tree every day.

May be, the confiscation – of every single electrical /engine run wood saw, as well confiscating every wood-logs carrying vehicle and a total ban on saw mills may improve the situation to some extent.

Needless to mention that the sales proceeds of the Tree planted by the forefathers of the Peasant in distress is very meager. Moreover the mill owners make fat sum by selling the sized wood to struggling citizen, who are out building shelters from their life time savings!

How ridiculous—but so REAL !

Deforestation endangers our planet like a tumor that wont spare anything living, including the vital micro soil fauna - almost overnight.

Merely triggering a worldwide drive for Tree Plantation—would be of no use if there be no water to nurse the saplings.

Conservation of water and adoption of sustainable measures for increasing the aquifer level should be given top priority.

Merely creating 'Farm-Ponds' with Poly-linings (Whose life is still at stakes) to benefit capitalist farmers is not a judicious approach to quench the thirst of the marginal dry land peasants.

Instead,-deepening of every micro &nano water ways in the proximity of the rural settlements all over and then filling it with coarse sand and boulders—would make more sense to harness the rain water rather resourcefully. This way at least the rural drinking water problem would definitely be solved. And if by god's grace—if the rains are pretty, then even the agricultural thirst would be quenched.

Other sustainable water saving measures, besides the capital oriented drip irrigation could be,

1. Capsule Growing (illustrated in a separate chapter)

2. Mulching of shredded bio mass in the vicinity of fruit / agro forestry tree trunks & covering it with appropriate size used news paper sheets and their subsequent sealing with thin mulch layer and fine top soil—has a good water saving effect in times of acute water scarecity. Mere, moistening the covered surface of the mulch layer by a back pack sprayer may be once a week, helps the survival of the plant in fruiting /flowering during a long dry spell.

3. Another sustainable measure is to make a circular trench of say 8" x 8" (width x depth) in the plants active root zone and then filling it with shredded bio mass like glericidia etc. before sealing it with the top soil .

Now if a stream of flow irrigation water is allowed to enter the sealed circular bio mass trench tangentially on diametrically opposite sides then likewise of the capillary action the desired flow of water rushes into the trench from either sides—keeping the plants root zone moist for several preceding weeks during the summer.

1. Similarly—if water flow channels are made against the slope of fruit / forestry plantations adjoining the tree trunks and about one meter length wise area in the basin of the water channel is dug on either sides of the tree trunk and subsequently filled with shredded bio mass and covered with soil to retain the original trough level, then as water flows, this acts as an accumulator to replenish water to the plants for longer periods particularly in the summer season.

   It is indeed more of common sense to conserve water and use it rather efficiently.

2. The 'Golden-Ridge' is yet another novel way to achieve bio diversity on the smallest farm holdings besides utmost water conservation, without adopting costly drip irrigation technologies.

These are some of the simple water saving techniques but then no one believes in simpler solution in this era of modern precision farming.

A time has come when diminishing returns in the wake of global warming would thrust the needy peasants to believe in these simple life loving doctrines.

Either now or never we all must understand that we now have hardly any chances to breathe fresh air!

The world wide awareness for the environmental protection has rendered agriculture to be the fulcrum of survival for the life on earth.

The Brazil Earth Summit of the 90's and the ever growing thrust on the national organic programs(NOP) has forced agriculture to take a greener turn once for all!

Surprisingly enough – all these years agriculture was like a free lance affair – with no ecological server, thus riding all of us into a man-made hell of the green house – effect.

Hopefully, now with the tightening of all corners for eco-farming the situation would soon improve.

Needless to stress that the *ENVIROMENTAL PROTECTION* has to be the only prosper theme of this millennium.

Now the point is that who could protect the environment more efficiently? Obviously the agriculturist alone! As the relation of agriculture and the ecology is like that of a husband and a wife. Just as the wife obeys the husband – the agriculturist must obey the nature!

It is so simple – yet so difficult, in the wake of increased number of divorces in these times.

FARMERS AND THE ECOLOGY

Although, I am a farmer – I must confess for being the greatest devastator of the eco- system. It is not intentional but for the ignorance, lack of vision and the reversal of age old farming traditions - to produce more and more from the same piece of land.

I still recollect the incidence of my childhood when the felling of tree in the process of bringing new land under cultivation hardly meant anything even to my father who was a respectable farmer.

Such thoughtless acts for years together has dragged each one of us in to such a catastrophically situation.

So it is high time – we condemn the childish behavior of our fore fathers and march ahead with a noble manifesto for the protection of the environment.

The young farmers must be educated to be the true custodians of the environment and make tree – plantation to be obligatory on the farming community in proportion of their holdings, in the days to come.

Farmers around the world have only mastered – reaping the soil, their restoration is still not in their school of thought.

Let us now restrict the greenification of our planet to the peasants and not rope in the urban folks – though they have truly focused the world's attention on the environmental issues.

It is the Peasants'self realization alone that would truly energise the ecological drive worldwide.

ECOLOGICAL RESTORATION IS NOT MAGICAL. . .

…….. But it sure is a miracle!

While agriculture boasts of a legendary heritage its recent hay and way drift in wake of mass production has now compelled us all to think about the

Mother – earth, than the, Agriculture itself!

To save the mother – earth from any more abuses – the peasants must spin the wheel of agriculture the other way round by inducting the following doctrines into their occupational matrix,

- ✦ Zero Tillage/ Minimum Tillage
- ✦ Production of health foods with the help of bio-manures and pest control supplements.
- ✦ Bio-diversity at all farm levels

Monasto Fukuoka of Japan has already kindled the torch of organic farming in the early 80's – we only have to keep it ablaze with an – attitudinal change.

It is not an impossible task. It would be rather joyous if we learn to obey the nature with more devotion and sincerity.

In this manner, we all sons of the soil would be unified into a single global village with the nature as the universal deity and Eco-Farming as the only anthem.

Eventually there would be no racial stigma.

No more Muslims or the Hindus, Christians & Buddhist etc.

……….it would only be a world of human beings with smiles and cheers of content.

How wonderful the world would be – if the peasants perform their occupation in tune with nature.

In nutshell – trees, forests and the greens would be the only rhymes of happiness in our life if we accept environmental protection to be our only religion.

Let the rustling wind dwindle the tiny tree shoots and the flower stems whistle to a natural note to resonate into our lives forever!

The author is busy grooming his age old chemical free farm into an ideal eco-tourism venture – 'Nature Station Aditya'. (The conceptual brochure could update on his craving for eco-farming and eco-tourism)

WELCOME
to NATURE STATION ADITYA
& EXPLORE THE UNEXPLORED !!

- Ancient Shukracharya Temples
  (Kach-Devyani legend) .. 07 kms
  Hingne wada reservoir .. 06 kms
- Ancient Mahadev Temple
  at Kumbhari .. 15 kms
- Sai Dham .. 03 kms
- Janardan Swami Temple .. 06 kms
- Jangli Maharaj Temple .. 09 kms
- Fort Ankai-Agasti Rishi Temple .. 28 kms
- Nandurmadhmeshwar
  Bird Sanctuary .. 50 kms
- Shirdi-Saibaba .. 25 kms
- Shani Shingnapur .. 70 kms
- Daulatabad Fort .. 100 kms
- Ellora caves .. 90 kms
- Ajanta Caves .. 195 kms
- Aurangabad .. 105 kms
- Nasik .. 90kms
- Ahmednagar .. 100 kms

RSVP: Suresh G. Kolhe

G. K. MEMORIAL CENTRE FOR NATURE CARE

Kolhe Niwas, Gurudwara Road, Near Bus Stand,
Kopargaon - 423 601, Dist. Ahmednagar,
Maharashtra (India). Ph: (02423) 23148

Nature Station Aditya is a small Kingdom in itself, only 25 Cms north of the world famous SAIBABA SHRINE at GHIRDI. Pilgrimmage apart, it is indeed a *gateway* into the rich industrial sugar-belt for businessmen, service-professions) & consultants to explore novel business avenues.

LOCATION-*Near village Yeogaon, only 15 km off the well-known National Highway NH-6*

PRINCIPAL TOWN-*Kopargaon (5 kms), the Sugar Capital of the country, on the banks of the Godavari River.*

NEAREST RLY STN.-*Kopargaon, on the Manmad-Daund broad gauge rail link.*

NEAREST AIRPORTS - *Aurangabad (Chikalthana) - 110 kms. Nashik 65 kms. Shirdi (proposed)-50 kms*

CLIMATE-*Warm Summers (Feb-June)*
COOL WINTERS-*(Nov-Feb)*)
RAINFALL-*20" (June to Nov.)*
(Mild Tropical climate all year round)

** Several sugar, paper & chemical factories, distilleries & fisheries are placed within 40 min. drive of Nature Station Aditya.*

with best Compliments

From,

Suresh Kolhe
B. E (M)

Nature Station Aditya would soon house hostel type accomodation & health food restaurant amidst a natural setting called - The Temple of Trees (Vijay Chakra).

Exclusive (chemical-free) lustrous Exotic Tropical Fruit & forestry plantations with several ponds, rippling streams, chanting birds and colourful butterflies intersperse the several fresh-air trails within - a feast for the young & old alike.

It also provides a unique opportunity for the investor-creators to transform their rich experience into noteworthy enterprise: merely by working in close proximity with Nature. Backed by a hi-tech. service workshop, Nature Stn. Aditya provides an ideal place for Nature lovers, Photographers, Film-makers, Executives , Designers, Businessmen and commercial establishments for conducting Management Workshops and 'Launching' ceremonies in an eco-friendly environment.

Nature Station Aditya is also a shoppers paradise for everything, from organic foodstuff to handicrafts.

Farming Philosophy —

) 'Each piece of land
is a Kingdom in itself
& the peasant is Toil &
Tilth in harmony with
Nature blossoms into
Happiness for all !

Entry view →
Pond laced with tropical lustre.

Nature Station
ADITYA
...for the Blend of Happiness in Life!

> Special Features & Announcements <

COMMUNITY FARMING-To enable urban enthusiasts to learn & rejoice the art of farming & animal care.

WORK-BAYS-(For artists/craftsmen & photographers) placed in a 'Natural Forest' environment, backed with appropriate infrastructure.

AMPHI-THEATER, *under a sacred grove,* with open conferencing facility- *for business services, cultural & religious ceremonies.*

ALSO: Yoga, Meditation & Herbal health care under expert guidance, so too guid foot excursion trails, bicycle trails, bullock cart trails (to nearby village), adventure trails to Fort Ankai & Nandurmadhmeshwar Bird Sanctuary.

Appropriate Farm mechanization — the key to save the environment !

CHAPTER 2

Capsule growing

Capsule Growing…….simple yet magical!

As a tribute to my toiling father, I decided to make some significant contribution to bring about sustainability into the agriculture of the tropics.

I was still confused as I was disabled and hardly had any money to blow – off in trials and experiments on the fields.

So what?

I knew only one thing – I had to do it and that was all!

Eventually the simple concept of capsule growing was inducted into bio-farming practice merely through an endless craving for the agricultural sustainability.

Now, with a mission in mind, every morning I used to go to the farm with the eureka of hopes.

Somehow the ever escalating weeds, the water scarcity and inadequate - inputs used to suppress my zeal at the end of each day.

Leaving me depressed once again. Obviously I slept restless nights all those years.

One fine morning of the early 1990's - I was sitting under a shady tree with my mind on the mission.

Helplessly – I closed my eyes for a few moments and surprisingly, I saw my father standing at the same spot where I had scattered my portion of his funeral ashes (we were five brothers)

This time he had shrugged – off the serious look from his face and sported a smile instead .I was very joyous and delighted and in the eagerness of walking towards him – I opened my eyes and despite of this day dream – I started looking for him.

I knew he wasn't there – anywhere!

……..but then I noticed a wild aromatic flower just blossoming from the entanglement of weeds on the very spot where my subconscious mind had spotted him only a few moments earlier.

I focused my mind deeper on the wild shrub that held this beautiful flower oozing natural fragrance all over. I soon – realized that several tiny buds were sprouting despite the fact that no one had particularly de weeded it's root zone nor fertigated or even watered it. Probably the Newtonian theory of enertia must have kept it going with the abundance of fauna in the bio rich soil beneath.

Suddenly – I seem to have found a solution to a very deep rooted problem but before the idea could be crystallized in my mind – the approaching farm worker – disturbed the chain of thought's – leaving me empty once again.

Later, for several weeks in the wilderness on the farm, I constantly thought of the following as to ……

……How could I increase the production area from the limited land that I hold?

……How could a small farmer like me eliminate the capitalist control – irrigation technology and the sophisticated farm mechanization and yet be at par with global competency? And,

…….How could I grow value added spices and herbs along with the routine food and fodder crops for added returns.

*……BESIDES CONTRIBUTING SIGNIFI CANTLY TO ERADICATE GLOBAL – WARMING …….**.through bio-diversity.***

It is indeed well said that necessity is the mother of invention and those days I always felt getting ever closer to the roots of disparity in agriculture.

Only a few days later – when I was busy planting just another sapling as usual – I casually glanced at those that I had planted the week earlier. I was shocked to notice that the weeds and the pests had – mercilessly entangled them all – leaving them nailed to the ground – stunting their growth once for all. Soon these unfortunate saplings would be drained out of life like SARITA's father RAMU.

I sensed that there is a flaw in my planting method itself. But how could it be? – As I obeyed the universal practice that almost every Peasant followed for ages together.

But then, I thought just as no one has any time these days even to look back – may be everyone planting saplings this way could be wrong too!

Any way, it is not a matter of debate – protection of the planted saplings was all that mattered to me at that juncture.

I knew, that the saplings must be protected from ,

✦ The leaching of water from their root zone,
✦ The harsh winds,
✦ The scorching sun,
✦ The entangling weeds,
……..only to name a few!

Now I was firm that whether, I find a proper solution or not – I would not plant the next sapling customarily as it had no provision to warrant the post emergence survival from the harshness of the nature.

So, I placed the sapling that, I held, under the shade of the neighboring shrub and sat peacefully thinking on overcoming this universal problem.

May be there was no possible solution at all. But again one thing was there for sure – the HOPE!

Now in order to avoid being philosophical - I diverted my mind by picking a stale folded news paper used as a cheap stuffing material in the corrugated paper box holding the nursery saplings.

I delicately unfolded the rusty news paper and curiously started browsing through the one time hot – head lines.

My mind was still wavering on the problem of reducing the post emergence plant mortality resourcefully and all of a sudden as if the heavens had bestowed on me – I realized that I was actually holding the solution of this age – old problem in my own hands.

"THE PIECE OF OLD NEWS PAPER"

What an idea?

I then had it cut into several pieces of different sizes and scrolled them into conical funnel like empty paper capsules,that's all!

Obviously, - nothing on earth could be cheaper and simpler remedy to such a tedious problem. *CAPSULE GROWING*, is certainly not a never heard concept to agriculture.

During my college days (in mid-1970's) in the historical city of Aurangabad (Near the world famous Ajanta and Ellora caves) – I used to be a radio fan. Listening particularly to, he VOA's breakfast show and the BBC's news round – ups.

It was the VOA's breakfast show that made me sport a smile for the whole of the day that followed.

How wise of *PAT GATES & PHIL IRWIN* to conduct the breakfast show with lots of smiles and slogans like,

"If you see someone without a smile,

Well, give him one of yours" !

I never dreamt those days - of meeting these wonderful hosts – someday. Later after a decade, I was overwhelmed with joy when, I met Pat and Phil in the VOA – studio in Washington DC during my first world tour in mid-1983. Coffee with them was memorable.

Down the memory lane – I also recollect out of the VOA'S informative sessions on agriculture those days (in mid of 1970's) when Phil Irwin jokingly said that the farmers of tomorrow would be firing the capsules of seeds and manure to cultivate their slopeylands.

Obviously, - he was focusing on the capsule – growing experiments being carried out by the USDA and the U.S. forestry department to bring some of the arid zones of Arizona and Nevada states under forestry plantations by firing the seed capsules prior to the preceding scanty rain showers on the slopey Terrain ahead.

The capsules made of ceramic clay contained vital elements of plant propagation in proper proportion viz.

+ The seed,
+ The manure,
+ The Super absorbents and the
+ Pest control coverings,

All, layered into concentric circles and then dried and cured.

All these entire bullet like capsules were then fired from the muzzle of the gun (similar to the smaller anti air-craft guns) from the firing ranges with timed intervals and angular deviations.

The parabolic trajectory scattered up these bullets haphazardly, plunging head on, into the sloppy terrain of the bio-scope.

Some days later – when the down pour would start, the elements in the capsules eventually triggered off the seed to life.

Over 30 % saplings from the capsules muzzled-off in this manner survived the harshness of the nature that persisted above the ground. It was merely due to their proper protection prior to their germination and thereof.

This was indeed a wonderful attempt to afforest a vast terrain with limited man power. A concept that truley deserves great salutes.

Fortunately – with the population exodus we are better off – with enough hands to greenify our horizon with innumerable trees and greens. But, again it is the matter of our attitude.

Thus joyously, holding the news paper in hand – I started unfolding the ideas that filled my mind a while before and simply started converting the newspaper cuttings into paper capsules.

It was the simplest form of capsule one could imagine and that too a workable one!

SHAPING OF IDEA INTO A CONCEPT →

The piece of rusty old news paper ascertained that it could be an ideal bio –degradable media to hold the seed inputs resourcefully - during the germination and the emergence period. This period is very crucial to the success of crop growing.

Without wasting any more time – I took a tapered axle – bar in hand and pierced it few inches deep into the moist soil and then slowly removed it by turning it around its own axis. It formed a taper hole into the soil – call it the **taper – socket**.

Now, all I needed was a taper plug/shank holding the seed / sapling – to be pushed snug fit into this taper soil socket.

How simple !

So – hastily, I simply tore 1/4th page of the old news paper and funneled it into a taper shaped hollow paper cone. Into this – I filled the adjoining top soil to the two thirds and then slowly rested a young sapling on to it and covered its roots and little part of its stem by ramming additional top soil around the base of the inserted young sapling.

Soon – the earlier hollow paper cone had turned into an eco – friendly solid capsule holding the tiny plant life in it. It was a life saving capsule for the sapling within.

The toughened paper plug with the young flower sapling – dancing on the gentle breeze was now ready for an inception into the soil socket formed earlier.

But before this placement – I had yet another idea for the plant protection. I took another ½ page of the old news paper – folded it four folds and tore a hole in the folded vertex, so the central hole could match/ align with the opening on the soil socket. I knew – with this the weeds protection problem could be eradicated besides immense saving in the irrigation water and the controlling of the root zone temperatures.

It was no more an idea but the *UREKA* to me !

So I spread the ½ size paper on the ground with its central hole on the opening of the soil socket and then slowly inserted the capsule into it. It was such a snug fit as if the capsule and the ground were of one matrix.

I then covered the news paper around the plug with deweeded dry trash and then covered it with good amount of top soil to bury the whole affair once and for all.

I knew this simple technique would warrant healthy propagation of the sapling even in the stormy winds and the blazing sun.

This was indeed a life line for the millions of toiling Peasants and it sure had the trick of a torpedo to blow off global warming once and for all.

Capsule growing methodology that I followed was on my farm – (now being groomed into *NATURE STATION ADITYA*) is simply narrated as under.

(ex. for planting of agro forestry from treated seeds/ sapling with the paper capsule method.)

1. Ensuring adequate stock of healthy seeds on hand prior to rainy season.

2. Ear marking of the plantation points and de - weeding a square foot of area around it pushing the resultant tiny heap of the debris and the scraped soil towards one end.

3. Allow few seasonal intermittent rainy showers to moisten, cool and soften the top soil – making it congenial for germinating the Seeds/Saplings inserted in the capsules

4. Subsequently make soil – socket on the earmarked plantation markings.
5. Then lay the ½ size newspaper page over the opening of the soil socket and insert the paper capsule (Holding the seed/sapling) into it.
6. Cover the paper around the plug with the de – weeded trash heap and bury it with some more top soil. That's all!

Now, even with the sparing showers – the seed / saplings triggers off to life and with few more showers the young sapling would nod with the gentle breeze – marking the happiest moments of my life!

This joy of appropriate waste recycling was indeed heavenly and it promised me of a smile on the face of the millions of toiling Peasants like my father who seldom smiled.

Somehow, if by misfortune the rains fail – then all we must do is to pour only 20ml to 30ml water on the mouth of the paper plug every week to ensure healthy growth of the sapling. This could be done manually on small scale by using used veterinary saline pouch, (It has the knob to moderate the flow.) and it could be easily strapped to the shoulders.

One may not believe but with only one gallon of water in hand – I have managed to support at least 100 saplings this way- without any other control irrigation measure.

No wonder – a school boy can easily plant 100 trees this way on a Sunday without getting exhausted.

Thus – with this young force available worldwide,we can easily win the war against global warming just within a decade or so.

To sum up – the agriculture in the tropics, with the smaller land holdings, could be made richer and joyous with such sustainable measures.

The field oriented drive is what is going to revolutionize the agriculture than a mere class room demo of the capsule growing concept.

I feel even, I am wasting my time by narrating my experience on the paper that is eventually going to decay someday – so instead why don't, I just scroll few bunches of old news papers and bring another hundreds of seeds to life!

So all in all – the capsule growing is virtually a penniless affair for zooming life on earth with resourceful eco-logical restoration.

Given a deeper thought – it could be the most resourceful–approach for the protection and preservation of rare medicinal / aromatic plant species that are on the verge of extinction.

- It is indeed more than a life line for peasants with smaller holdings and only handful of resources,
- It makes large/small scale mass tree plantation a reality thus restoring ecology in the shortest span of time.
- It takes the concept of waste recycling truly to the grass root level transforming – agriculture into a green sink.

CHAPTER 3

The Golden Ridge

– A hope for the millions of toiling Peasants!

Having successfully nursed - few saplings on the capsule growing concept -the main hurdle was its commercial application to benefit the masses.

So I kept on thinking on these lines for several days but only to be frustrated at the end of those restless days!

But somehow there was a reckoning within – that hinted, of my close proximity to the resourceful solution to this global problem. I felt that may be I had already won half the battle. But that was not enough.

In this quest for an appropriate solution to make farming ever sustainable – inquisitively, I started interrogating myself on the following grass root approach to agriculture,

- How could, I increase the plantation area from my smaller farm holding?
- How could, I be able to full-fill all my food and fodder needs from this holdings while growing some value added herbs and spices for slipping some additional dimes into my pockets?
- How could, I promote bio-diversity on my small farm – to combat Global Warming?

And moreover how could I achieve this rather economically.

It sounded like asking for the whole of the universe to be at your door steps. However finding a resourceful solution certainly emphasized on

Zero Tillage theory,

And lesser dependence on capital intensive input of the modern times viz. Control Irrigation &farm mechanization etc.

As a serious effort in resolving this issue - I decided to tackle those points one by one. I was confident of a proper solution as I already had the triumph card (Capsule Growing) in my pockets.

Hopefully – I looked at the sun but it wasn't easily seen as it were the mid day sun – blazing heat on my head. Besides ,Iwas hungry, so I left the farm and started riding my bike homewards. The glare of the way side newly laid tin-sheet roof of my neighbors dairy shed – irritated me as my grafted corneas couldn't take these refractions any longer. Apparently the convexity of the shiny – corrugated G.1. Roof sheets were making the glare unbearable for me in the hot afternoon.

Just like the miracle of the piece of old news paper several weeks earlier – the corrugation of the G.1. Sheets – sparked yet another idea in my mind to integrate capsule growing into the bio-diversity farming pattern that, I had in mind.

The corrugations would cover more surface area over the same stretch of land and this topography would increase the productive farming area.

It was yet another miracle and so, I named it as the ,

GOLDEN RIDGE TO PROSPERITY

Even at this juncture – I didn't have the slightest idea that within few days – I would be actually standing on the golden ridges with the paper capsule in hand to greet every peasant in distress, with bundles of hope. I then closed my eyes for a few minutes and was stunned to see Ramu holding a brand new slate in his hand. I knew for sure that there would be **no more broken slate** hence forth.

The next hurdle was – how to conserve irrigation water without the support of capital oriented Control irrigation measures.

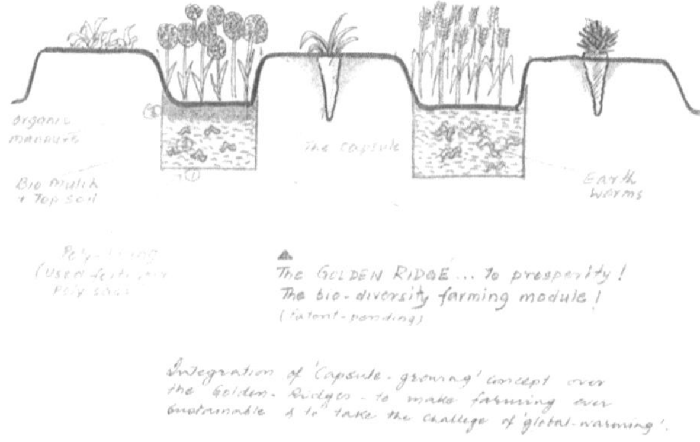

First, I started making corrugations/ ridges on the leveled land by digging two feet wide and one and a half feet deep trench manually. The excavated top soil was heaped on both the sides of the trench to form the RIDGES. These ridges, eventually constituted of two thick layers of rich top soil (one original layer and the other the excavated top soil of the trench).

When, I stepped out of the trench and glanced at the corrugations/ ridges – I literally got scared of the mess, I had made on my traditional field.

I felt depressed again and helplessly sat on a used fertilizer poly – bag under the shade of the nearby mango tree.

As I looked deeply onto the used fertilizer bag - yet another thought pierced my mind. It was indeed an hatric of miracles for me. I felt myself to be the richest person on the earth and within moments, I was day- dreaming to reach for the SKIES.

What a joyous feeling indeed!

The woven poly-sacs are generally used as a packing material for some of the basic NPK fertilizers all over the world. As such the used poly sacs are available in plenty and they pose environmental threat too and they have no commercial value and they have no provision for recycling.

The 50kg sacks are of universal dimension. They are all 21" wide which was very important to me. I knew this width could very easily make the woven fabric slip into the two feet wide trench – solving the water conservation problem once for all.

I immediately gathered couple of used poly sacs and tore them apart lengthwise from both sides. Then I stitched several such sacks together to form a long stretch of 21" wide woven sack film.

I then rolled this film in a cylindrical roll and slowly started laying it along the length of the trench.

Simultaneously – I started covering the spread fabric, with 3 to 4 inches of freshly dug soil layer from the trench bottom itself.

With the poly membrane disappearing into the soil – the trench bottom obviously remained lined with the cost effective poly sack liner. It was yet another judicious gimmick of waste recycling.

This I feel was the greatest achievement in curtailing drip irrigation and that too so simply!

The subsequent operations were of routine type viz.

1. Filling the trench with field wastes (de weeded trash) and manure to the mouth of the trench.

2. Inducting these above layers with decomposing bacteria,Super phosphate and EM-Strains etc. during the filling operation (These were all in situ inputs)

Finally – using a regular 35h.p. farm – tractor – I flattened the ridges to form raised beds by thrusting the excess top soil back into the trenches.

The whole pattern now looked like an engineering marvel – the earlier heap of soil (the ridges) now looked chiseled into perfect flat – beds like the ones used for the propagation of seeds and sapling in agro – nurseries. I knew they would provide an ideal raised bed for integrating the capsule growing concept on them.

All put together – they would fetch more than gold to the millions of toilers on the field – some day!

OBIVIOUSLY – *THESE WERE THE GOLDEN RIDGES TO ME.*

now, prospering with this typical non conventional farming pattern was the final challenge for me.

There were several options that came to my mind like-

- ✦ Planting of appropriate crop and plant species to promote bio-diversity while producing food / fodder and spices simultaneously in one location.

OR

Even go for fruit. . . meadow orchard,

Herbs and spices combinations

OR

Cotton and Onions or Sugar Cane & Gram etc.

There could be limitless permutations like that of the kaleidoscope.

It was a small beginning of a new revolution on my farm.

To start with – I used the capsule growing technique to implant young teak, coriander and cinnamon sapling on the ridges at 12', 3' & 12' linear spacing resp. i.e. a plant at every yard along the length on the ridges. I still had the trench vacant to plant something else. In the first trench I planted onion, in the second one I planted -

Wheat and Garlic in the third.It was like the Ali-baba's treasure – I could plant anything from ginger, gram, or even sugar cane in the subsequent trenches.

Self sufficiency of food / fodder and spices would no longer be a dream for peasants with marginal land holdings – if they farm over the golden ridges with utmost seriousness and sincerity.

To make such bio – diversity so easily achievable, all I had to do was to flood irrigate the trenches at different intervals as per the crops –water requirement.

The woven sack membrane beneath the trench functioned like a check valve, almost forcing the flood water to percolate sideways more freely than leaching below the crop's root zone

This natural lateral spread of water provided an ideal field condition for the saplings implanted on the ridges. They would soon make an – healthy emergence from the capsules in to the horizon. Further – the flooding of the trenches provided added humidity for the healthy growth of the spices / herbs on the ridges the days to precede.

Subsequently, the vigor of the teak and the aroma of coriander and cinnamon finally quenched my soul that was restless for so long.

Soon,
- ✦ The tender sparkling leaves,
- ✦ The glazing stems
- ✦ The sprouting buds
- ✦ The interpersing of the bees and the butterflies and the aroma of the,
- ✦ Humus rich soil...

...literally drove me beyond heavens!

It was like something in several hundreds of lives – sacred than the holiest of the rituals. For me it was an end of all askings. An ultimate joy to last forever.

The golden ridges – simply provided a full stop to several conventional agricultural crop production practices like,

+ The deep ploughing,
+ Frequent de – weeding and intercultivation,
+ Precise watering and fertilization,
+ Frequent agro – chemical sprays for plant protection etc.

The golden ridges were destined to yield without exerting much for years to follow. Just harvest the trenches, pluck the ridges, then rake the top soil and simply broadcast fresh crop seed over the trench and let it go on, and on like a roulette in the casino - That's all!

The rich and the abundant top soil would induce the seeds to germinate by itself likewise the flywheel of an engine that rotates effortlessly after the initial jerk.

With this reality – I had the full might, to spin the wheel of agriculture the other way around.

I wish Ramu was still alive to see it all happen so easily. As a tribute to his unfortunate soul – I carried home a brand new slate and hooked it on the wall hanger. I then took a piece of chalk and scribed the three words on it,

"FOR RAMU'S SARITA"

That day was the end of a gruelling journey for me. It was miles away from the dead end!

No one could be ever happier than me and I was desperate to share the joy with everyone on the planet.

I am sure the golden ridge would be a key to make this happen for sure. The simple doctrine evolved out of struggle through hard times had the strength to make every toiling peasant trail back from the dead end.

The bio diversity farming pattern of the golden ridges could be a bench mark for the graduating ecologists and the nature lovers for decades to follow.

What more one could expect from a very small piece of land. Truly – if each one of us religiously adapts this sustainable bio farming system then within months the vegetation would be flocked with bees, butterflies and the birds – making this very earth a heaven for us all !

To sum up – the salient features of the golden ridge bio diversity farming pattern are →

1. Zero tillage
2. Utmost water conservation
3. Year round harvest for years together.
4. Super intensive farming
5. Increased cultivable area
6. Supports – supportive farming like bee – keeping, silk rearing etc.
7. Holds good for any farm size.
8. Ideal for several cash crops like sugarcane, cotton, onion, rice & wheat etcin these hard times of inflation
9. It creates congenial micro-climate to produce FOOD/FODDER AND SPICES simultaneously

10. It is economical as it optimizes labour utilization

11. It creates enormous job – opportunities for working hands.

12. The eco friendly nature and the bio diversity fauna provides better comfort level and stress free working environment for the labourers.

Lastly it bridges the gap between mankind and the nature while combating GLOBAL WARMING resourcefully!

CHAPTER 4

Eradication of Global Warming - The dream!

NOW OR NEVER !

GLOBAL WARMING

"Let us not talk about it, - Let us eradicate it!"

As the role of agriculture is very crucial in tackling this issue – the Peasants must line-up in front,to wage a war against global warming – just like the artillery and the grenadiers in the surface combat!

Obviously – global warming has to be seriously fought like a battle. In fact we all have to be at war against global warming and that too right now!

It is not impossible,

nor,

Something unaffordable like the nuclear warfare !

All we have to do is to create as many water ponds and lace them with as many trees around.

Will it not be ever simpler with the golden ridge – circumscribing these revolutionary ponds in contour like manner?

It is really hard to believe that such an alarming issue could be so easily tackled.

We are already late, let us not wait anymore. Let us all unfold the old news papers and integrate the capsule growing concept on the golden ridge to let every pond in our vicinity blossom again.

Once we are through with the bio – diversity plantation – the eco system could automatically take on the baton of this relay of survival from us and soon bring happiness in to our life.

Remember – the nature is undefiable and has the strength and means of winning every battle.

There are several aspects of which I know a little but all the same they are significant in our war against global warming.

Global warming cannot be tackled by ecological restoration alone but also by promoting healthy and pure vegetarian diet for all of us on this planet.

Vegetarian diet is a balanced diet and super intensive bio farming alone would be able to feed the ever growing number of mouths on the planet- earth !

❖-❖-❖

While the severity of global warming is on the rise – to live up to it - necessitates for toughening ourselves. By all means – we must increase the immunity in us – which is possible only by adopting the YOGIC way of life. The regular cycle of yogic kriyas like pranayama would not only ensure good health but would also warrant mental peace and happiness.

In the good old days - the hard working Peasants were looked up on as the symbol of fitness by the rest of the world.

Post war devastation and the consequent birth of hybridization, has even made these sweating peasants equally sick and unhealthy.

The harmful narcotic chain tightening into the grass roots has also succeeded in engulfing the farming folks ! Many peasants have died by frequent – chewing of tobacco on hungry stomachs.

So to say – while producing health food for the planet the Peasants should not succumb to vices like tobacco, beedi, cigarette, liquor etc.

They must resolve to induct yoga and naturopathy diet into their lives hence forth without recourse.

Let me caution again that as the Medicare is getting dearer day by day – it would be ever difficult for the Peasants with limited resources to get hospitalized in the event of serious health problems. They would be compelled to make up to it via the money – lenders dens – thus once again falling into a trap with hardly any way out.

Sad to focus on the grim reality, that most of the marginal farm fraternity heads- still can't afford the sanitary pads for their maturing daughters or the newly wedded daughters in law.

How could they afford costly hospitalization?

They have to adhere to simple precautionary, affordable health measures to keep health disorders at an arm's length hence forth.

Farmers often carry a wrong notion of fitness in view of their hard physical labour for most of the day. But if we closely observe their body movements – they are usually unidirectional as far as the movements of the back bone or the spinal chord are concerned. It is only the compreshive spinal yogic asana'sthat would de-stress their stressed up spinal vertebrates in a natural manner. The yogic exercises are very vital to them in order to avoid rather serious disorders with the advent of age.

Now in order to face global warming, higher immunity levels should be attained which can only be accomplished through the Yogic way of life. (The warrior has to be trough first, to fight a battle).

Conclusion

Lastly with, the race to rope in the marginal farmers into Farm-mechanization – the risk of borrowings would be higher.

Also like most of the Peasants – my father too had very less – knowledge of machinery &equipments and as a consequence – he had his hard earned money simply blown, to fall into the trap of sweet tounged mechanics who were offered handsome kickbacks from the town traders who sold spurious Tractor parts/lubricants etc at exorbitant prices. The Engine reconditioning shops in the cities also had their own billing pattern – to cover the mechanics.

All these, left the farmers with machinery, virtually bankrupt before the next sowing season.

So to say – there should be authorized Farm mechanization parts selling shops with monitoring on their prices as well the Peasants should be given crash courses on the maintenance of farm M/c and equipments they are using, to avoid such disasters arising out of shere innocence of the illiterate Peasants.

They should be warned that innocence is not at all an excuse in today's world.

+ Crash courses on repairs and maintenance of electric motors and starters would also be crucial.

+ Making good quality farm equipments promptly available on reasonable rent for the small and medium farmers-would be a dire necessity to bring sustainability.

To sum up in order of improving agricultural sustainability and to prevent miseries like Ramu's demise – the government could rope in some large Industrialists, NGO's and even the able military man power to mass produce under mentioned products viz,

1. 3 HP Motor Pump Set with Suction/Delivery and Starter assemblies, Electric Cables & Submersibles.

2. Janata Model, basic insecticide/Pesticide & Fungicide Formulations.

3. Agri Tools & Tackles like Shovels, Crowbars and other vital hand tools.
4. Low (03)h.p. Portable cold storage chests.
5. Refer Van – goods carriers upto 1 MT capacity/ (refer Van rickshaws)
6. Waste recycled bio-manures
7. Bicycles, Dhoti's& Cotton Sari's &Shirting's.
8. Hi-tech, Pre-digester type Bio – Gas plants to produce methane gas for energy.
9. Basic human and veterinary Medicines & so on
10. Low h.p. Power – Weeders, Sprayers and Seed Drills for better crop protection.
11. Production of Bio-diesel from Plant Species etc.
12. Development of small backpack electrostatic sprayers to reduce spray volumes in Agriculture (Thus reducing the use of harmful Agro-Chemicals)
13. Development of efficient Gasifiers to produce in-situ electricity from agricultural prunnings and wastes.

These could be offered to Farming/Other working communities thro' special Kissan-Malls on no-profit, no-loss basis to help the peasants sustain. Eventually, lots of people would get jobs.

Above all there is a dire necessity for harnessing the blazing tropical sun for alternate energies to benefit the tiny farm community.

Viz.-

✦ Solar cum Wind, Hybrid Water Lifting Pumps.

✦ Solar driers – for dehydration of Vegetables & fruits.

✦ Solar backed tiny cold storage chests

✦ Solar Lighting for illuminating the farm dwellings.

✦ Wood chippers & Shredders to feed appropriate Gasifiers for production of in-situ electricity on the farms.

(These are only to name a few!)

Such technologies would certainly induct sustenance in to the distressed farm community for years together.

– Suresh Kolhe

CHAPTER 5

The Festive Aura of Agriculture

The festive aura of Agriculture

It is perhaps for these happy moments, the roulette of agriculture has been spinning for centuries together.

These festivities alone infuse joy into the agony studded lives of the toiling peasants.

In fact the festivities of agriculture add colors to every ones lives.

They have a true significance with the agriculture itself. As agriculture is a year round activity, these festivals are also celebrated throughout the year signifying particular farming occasion.

It is perhaps for these cultural reasons – this holy occupation is named as AGRI-CULTURE!

The most popular Agricultural festivities along with their significance in nutshell could be narrated as under,

(Nagapanchami)

The festival of Baisakhi

Or Pongal in East is similar

To the thanks giving or

The turkey day of the West

In addition to these foremost festivals the other Indian agriculture festivals are

Nagapanchami is a sacred Indian festival dedicated to the Snake-God. The festival gets its name from the fact that it is celebrated on the fifth day (panchami) of the moonlit fortnight of the Hindu month of Shravan (July / August). According to the Gregorian calender, the festival is observed sometime in August.

WatPournima is celebrated in the month of Jesht (May-June). Women observe a fast and tie threads around a banyan tree and pray for the same husband in every birth. The celebration derived from the story of Savitri and Satyavan. It has been foretold that Satyavan won't live long. Resting on

the lap of Savitri, Satyavan was waiting for death under a banyan tree, when the day of death comes. The messenger of Yama, the God of death came to take Satyavan. But Savitri refused to give her beloved husband. Messenger after messenger tried to take Satyavan away, but in vain. Finally, Yama himself appeared in front of Savitri and insisted to give her husband.

KojagiriPoornima or AshwinPoornima is celebrated on the full moon day of Ashwin (September-October). As the rainy season passes, the sky becomes clear and the moon shines in the sky with full brightness. So, it is the celebration of this occasion, which is very traditional. It is

also known as the Kaumudi, meaning moonlight.

Pongal is an ancient festival of people in South India particularly Tamils. The history of the festival can be traced back to the Sangam Age i.e. 200 B.C. To 300 A.D. Although, Pongal originated as a Dravidian harvest festival and has a mention in Sanskrit Puranas, historians identify the festival with the **Thai Un** and **Thai Niradal** which are believed to have been celebrated during the Sangam Age.

Balipratipada is the half auspicious moments. During a calendar year, there are some inauspicious days, and some days have both or only one aspect. If one performs certain important acts such as wedding, buying properties, etc. during auspicious time, then that act proves to be beneficial. The three and a half auspicious days are such that one can perform any act during the entire day because every moment of these days is auspicious.

AkshayaTritiya is traditionally celebrated as the birthday of the Hindu sage Parashurama, the sixth Avatar (incarnation) of the god Vishnu. According to Hindu mythology, on this day the Treta Yuga began and the river Ganges, the most sacred river of India, descended to the earth from the heaven.

Onam, the annual harvest festival is an occassion of great joy. Celebrated mainly in the Indian state of Kerala, the Onam celebrations range from four days to ten days, and centre around worshipping, music, dances, sports, boat races and of course...delicious foods. The festival originates from various legends and traditional beliefs.

Happy
Bhogi Festival

Bhogi festival is the first day of Pongal and is celebrated in honor of Lord Indra, "the God of Clouds and Rains". Lord Indra is worshiped for the abundance of harvest, thereby bringing plenty and prosperity to the land. Thus, this day is also known as Indran. On Bhogi all people clean out their homes from top to bottom, and collect all unwanted goods.

MakarSankranti is among the most auspicious occasions for Hindus and is celebrated in almost all parts of India. It is a harvest festival and is celebrated in many cultural forms with immense devotion, fervor and cheerfulness. The festival is celebrated on 14th January and is possibly the only Indian festival whose date always falls on the same day each year with just a few exceptions.

Lohri, a *seasonal festival of North India* is as old as that of story of Indus Valley civilization itself. The Festival of *Lohri marks* the end of winter and the coming of spring and the new year. The fires lit at night, the hand warming, the song and dance and the coming together of an otherwise atomized community, are only some of the features of this festival.

Bihu, with a lot of delight and joviality. The carnival which is celebrated with passion and vehemence marks the change of season. The history of the significant and noteworthy celebration dates back to 3500 B.C. At that point, it was one month long celebration. However, today it is celebrated thrice a year and each time for a week.

Jallikattu is based on the simple concept of "flight or fight". Cattle being herd and prey animals in general tend to run away from unwanted situations. But there are quite noteworthy exceptions. Cape buffalos are famous for standing up against lions and killing them. The Indian Gaur bull is known for standing its ground against predators and tigers think twice about attacking a full grown Gaur bull. Aurochs, the ancestor of domestic cattle was known for its pugnacious nature. Jallikattu bulls belong to a few specific breeds of cattle that descended from the kangayam breed of cattle and these cattle are very pugnacious by nature. These cattle are reared in huge herds numbering in hundreds with a few cowherds tending to them. These cattle are for all practical comparisons, wild and only the cowherds can mingle with them without any fear of being attacked. It is from these herds that calves with good characteristics and body conformation are selected and reared to become jallikattu bulls. These bulls attack not because they are irritated or agitated or frightened, but because that is their basic nature.

Pola is a festival related to bull-worshiping and celebrated by farmers generally in Maharashtra state in India. Pola comes in Shravana month on PithoriAmavasya day which is also called the new moon day. This is mainly celebrated in Vidharbha region. This is the special day for farmers. On this occasion, the farmers' first give bath to their bullocks, decorate them with ornaments and worships them. In the evening, the parade of decorated bulls carried out with music and dance across the village. Perhaps, India is the only country in the world, where people celebrate festivals to pay respect to the animals also.

Baisakhi marks the time for harvest of Rabi (winter) crops and is therefore extremely significant for the farmers. Baisakhi Festival is also celebrated as a Thanksgiving Day festival in these states. After waking up early and dressing themselves in new clothes, farmers visit temples and gurdwaras to express gratitude to God for the good harvest and seek blessing for ensuing agriculture season. Farmers also celebrate Baisakhi by performing energetic bhangra and gidda dance and participating in **Baisakhi Fairs.**

Above all , is the festival of DIPAVALI Also known as the festival of lights, It is celebrated for almost a fornight durring october end & the first week of November of every year . It is celebrated by one and all - The Traders as well the farming community.

The enlighting of hundreds of natural cooking oil lit lamps into each house on the dark eve of the Amavasya commemorates the Victory of the good over the Evil and the beginning of a new era of Peace and Happiness.

Thanks Giving day

In 1621, the Plymouth colonists and Wampanoag Indians shared an autumn harvest feast that is acknowledged today as one of the first Thanksgiving celebrations in the colonies. For more than two centuries, days of thanksgiving were celebrated by individual colonies and states. It wasn't until 1863, in the midst of the Civil War, that President Abraham Lincoln proclaimed a national Thanksgiving Day to be held each November.

ABOUT MYSELF

(…I truly know not much!)

Name - Suresh Genuji Kolhe

Age - 64 Yr. (01.05.1952)

Address - Kolhe Niwas, Gurudwara raod ,

Author in his forty's

Beginning of the mission

Kopargaon – 423601 (M.S.)

Mb. 8275451826

Mail – sureshkolhe@gmail.com

Education - An Engineering graduate with obession for Natural Farming !

Experience - Born & brought up in an Agriculturalist's family of repute. I was lucky to make two world tours in 1983 & 1984 adding enormously to my fields of interests. viz. – Appropriate farm Mechanization & Control irrigation technologies

- Bio-Farming & Harvesting the sun for alternate energies

- Eco Tourism (Nature Station Aditya)

My Farming Philosophy-

"Each piece of land is a kingdom in itself – where the peasants toil & till in harmony with nature blossoms into happiness for all!"

Hobbies – Singing, Poetry, Getting along with People and Travelling.

My, forthcoming books :

1. "The Saint with the rusted throne' (A synopsis's of the spiritual-teachings of the self less Saint late Janardan Swamiji)

2. A poetic album in HINDI 'Dil ke Jharokhnse' (. . . . Reflections of the various facets of life)

A staunch bio-farmer with over 3-decades of grass root experience. Presently busy transforming my 'chemical-free farm' into an Eco Tourism venture 'Nature Station Aditya'.

*(The Author is visually handicapped as he has grafted both of his eyes with donor cornea's).

Bibliography

1. **Bio –diversity** – A farming pattern , – contained and laced with several plant species of varied nature, like the ones found in the natural forests.
2. **De- salination** – A process for the conversion of Brakish / Saline Sea water into portable water safe for drinking purpose.
3. **Eco-tourism** – A nature friendly tourism activity on a farm converted into tourist paradise without disturbing the farming culture.
4. **Formula Racings** – a courageous motor – sport on specially prepared racing – tracks – for speed and endurance, using specially built formula racing cars.
5. **Gasifiers** – A pressure vessel used for the partial combustion of hog-fuel to generate producer gas (used as fuel energy for various purposes).
6. **Green – sink** – A lush green forest amidst the river basin/mountain troughs or around large,lake vicinities.
7. **Hot rodding/Drag Racing/Stunt-driving** – A typical life risking motor – sport depicting extra ordinary courage of the driver & the men behind the machines.
8. **Mono – culture** – Extensive farm lands with single cropping pattern.

9. **Holocaust–**

   1. A great or complete devastation or destruction - especially by fire.

   2. The systematic mass- slaughter of Jews in the Nazi concentrationcamps of theWorld War II.

10. **Power-Weeder** – A small engine driven rotary tilling device to de-weed post emergence soil around the pre planted zone.

11. **Rallying** – A typical long loop endurance race on difficult terrain using ordinary stock-cars.

12. **Refer – van** – A portable refrigerated container fitted on vehicle chassis preferably using the vehicles engine power.

13. **Wood chipper** – A device to prepare shredded hog – fuel from several wood category farm wastes (like Orchard/Vineyard prunnings etc.).

www.ingramcontent.com/pod-product-compliance
Lightning Source LLC
Chambersburg PA
CBHW051454250726
48655CB00001B/400